TREASURES
of
GOD

Experiencing God's Blessings

As We Go Through Trials,
There Will Always be Treasures

Jane S. Cochran

5 Fold Media
Visit us at www.5foldmedia.com

Treasures of God

Published by 5 Fold Media, LLC
www.5foldmedia.com

ISBN:978-0-9827980-4-1

Cover design by Cathy Sanders @ 5 Fold Media

Dedication

Dedicated to my Heavenly Father, Jesus and Holy Spirit, My Triune God. They are my companions, actually best friends. I must partner with them to bring in any fruit from this harvest.

On this journey I want to give recognition to Edward W. Cochran, my loving husband deceased in May of 1997. He instilled love, devotion, trust, guidance and protection in all I did. Our life together in marriage was fifty-three precious years, producing three children and along with their spouses, eight grandchildren.

Since my vision and dream with God, I have a joy and excitement in executing this book. I can't believe I am saying this, but God is loving and persistent with getting what He wants done. I am grateful for that or this book would have never come forth. I am truly leaning heavily on my precious Lord.

I know He gives me thoughts and words, strategies and guidance as needed. Do I ever need them? Of course! Each Christian has a job to do, a role to take or a contribution to make. Everyone's assignments, big and little, are necessary to carry out God's plans for His church and for the world (*I Cor. 12:12-28*). We are to be available to God by being active in His service. We are to help others, not just by being apostles, prophets or teachers (*Eph 4:11-12),* but by using spiritual gifts, such as healing or miracles (*I Cor. 12: 1-12)*. Every word in the Bible is inspired by God (*II Tim 3:16).*

God, our Heavenly Father, gave us this beautiful world and our precious Jesus. Father God always points to His only begotten Son, Jesus Christ. Jesus truly is the Way, the Truth, the Life in every avenue and the only way to the Father God. Holy Spirit maneuvers all directions. In the beginning God spoke the world into existence and was hovering over its surface (*Gen. 1:1,2).* Through Holy Spirit, God reveals the living Word, Jesus, to us. Every word in the Bible is inspired by God and is useful to teach us what is true and to make us realize what is wrong in our lives (*II Tim 3:16).* It is like a complete road map for living life. His word teaches and prepares us in every way and makes us fully equipped for blessings that God has in store for us.

I refer to the Bible as God's Word as this is first of all God's Book. This is one way He has led me. Keep your Bible close at hand and look up scriptures. You will be so blessed to do so.

Contents

Introduction to My Life

Introduction to My Life

I want to dedicate this book to my dear husband "Ed"- Edward Wareham Cochran. We grew up together by attending Miss Helen Hoffman's kindergarten that was housed across the street from Ed's home and three doors from my father's and grandparent's home.

Ed and I attended Junior High School at Woodland Way. We were attracted to each other in the 9th grade. We were both on the school tennis team, playing as partners at times. We dated through High School and College, knowing at our final graduation we would be married.

The war intervened and all male college students had to leave their school and enter the service. Ed was pursuing an aeronautical engineering degree at MIT and was in his junior year when he had to leave.

We were able to get married when Ed graduated from OCS (Officers Training School). Fortunately, we were able to be together during his entire time in the service. He was first stationed in Miami, FL then at Buffalo, NY. We then went to Reno, NV to live for a year and a half where Ed repaired damaged warplanes. After serving his time in the military, we returned to Boston for Ed to complete his degree. Our first son, Edward, Jr. was born there.

Ed and I were ardent church members and loved our Lord fervently. We had fifty-three years of a wonderful marriage with three children. Our first child, Edward Jr. was born in 1946 in Boston. Our second son, Robert was born in 1949 in Hagerstown, MD, and our third child, Susan was born in 1952, in Hagerstown.

We have eight grandchildren. Edward and his wife, Kate, had a daughter, Kristen, born in 1980, and a son, Matthew, born in 1983. Rob & his wife, Suzanne, had four children. Their first child, Elizabeth (Betsy), was born in 1979, their second child, Robert (Robbie), was born in 1982, their third child Christina (Chrissy), was born in 1989, and their fourth child, Anne (Annie), was born in 1993. Our daughter Susan was married to Kenneth in 1974. Susan married her second husband, Lonnie, in July 1987. Her first daughter, Rebecca, was born in 1980, and her second daughter, Lindsey, was born in 1989.

My father's father was Daniel A. Stickell. Daniel, (known to his friends as "D. A.") was not born in Hagerstown, but it was here that he prospered and became a well known businessman and civic leader. Born in Pennsylvania in 1860, he came to town at the young age of fourteen and worked as a miller for the Morning Star Mill. He later worked at the J. H. Gambrill Mill in Frederick, and also spent time working as a miller in Ohio. Stickell returned to Hagerstown and in 1883 rented the Andrew Hager Mill located in Hager Park. In 1896 he built the Stickell Mill on West Baltimore Street. He continued to mill grain at that location until a fire in 1929 destroyed it. After the fire, Mr. Stickell concentrated on mixing and making feed grain. His products were so popular that in 1945 he built a new mill to meet the demand. Years later when the mill was sold, the machinery was bought by the new state of Israel. Stickell gave generously of his time, serving on the boards of

Hood College, Mercersburg Academy, Washington County Hospital and as an elder at Zion Reform Church. When the plans for the YMCA were proposed, he worked hard to ensure the success of the project. Mr. Stickell was also a board member of the Hagerstown Bank that Jonathan Hager founded. When the Hagerstown Bank merged with the Maryland Surety Company in 1933 to form Hagerstown Trust, Mr. Stickell continued to serve as a board member. He died in 1952 at the age of 92. He still has family members residing in Hagerstown.

As I write this book, I want to put our Lord's words first then give my story. Occasionally a question arises in me, *are you capable to do this book?* Then I hear the Lord say, "*Is anything too difficult for Me?*" I hope each one who reads my stories will begin to understand God's untapped power can be hidden within them. You, too, can be given a dominating request, so beware!

I asked the Holy Spirit to lead and I would follow. His word is so important, so precious. Whoever is reading this book, have your Bible available to look up the scriptures listed, and read prayerfully. Chew on Psalms 1-2. It seems all one has to do is stand before God with a prepared and willing heart and let Him do His work. I claim II Cor. 12:9 that God's grace is sufficient for me, His power is made perfect in my weaknesses. For when I am weak, He is strong. I can boast more gladly about my weaknesses so that Christ's power may rest on me.

Chapter 1
My Calling

Chapter 1
My Calling

My ministry as a soul winner is to win the lost over to God's plan of salvation so they will receive Jesus Christ as their personal Savior. Then they are guaranteed a home in heaven.

The moment of salvation, you are truly born again. When you receive Jesus Christ in your mind and heart. You are cleansed from all sins as you surrender them completely to your Lord. Ask Jesus to come live in your heart to stay. You will not want to sin now and if you do make a mistake, ask Jesus to forgive you. God places His Holy Spirit in you now. Holy Spirit is your Friend, Director, Comforter, Counselor, Helper, Guide, Corrector, Teacher and Strengthener. The Holy Spirit is a personality; never a thing. He reveals Jesus to our heart.

Romans 10:9 says that if we confess with our mouth Jesus is Lord and believe in our heart that God has raised Him from the dead, we will be saved. It's that easy!

Galatians 3:26 says that we are now children of God by faith in Jesus Christ. The Holy Spirit reveals God's faith into your heart. You will now have a desire to share this faith with others so they, too, will one day live in heaven.

This process you have just begun is one you must make as God never forces us to accept Jesus as our Savior. You must exchange your sins for Jesus' righteousness. This is a definite divine transaction. Don't keep any unforgiveness now towards anyone. Give it all to Jesus. Jesus' shed blood provided deliverance when He rose alive from the grave through the power of God's Spirit (*Rom. 8:11).* Our trials that we go through bring treasures from God.

I need to confess why I am writing this book. I'm certainly not qualified to write a book. In February '08, I attended a three day Christian ministries seminar held by Brian and Pam Lake at the Plaza Hotel in Hagerstown, MD. Brian, Pam, and their children were there, along with Jill Austin, who was a teacher, preacher and prophet. Brian's pastor, Bill Chilcote was also ministering.

This was the third year I had attended their meetings here in Hagerstown. I found myself swept up in the presence of God at these encounters. Thursday evening was the first night all attendees were up front and being prayed for.

Jill Austin was teaching and prophesying to many of us there. As I was returning to my seat, Jill came up behind me and said, "God wants you to write a book about your stories." I thought, *no way would I do that*, and quickly put it out of my mind. Jill was supposed to fly the next day to minister at another seminar, but due to inclement weather, her flight was canceled. As a result, we had the privilege of having her minister to us again. Jill had "words" from God for many of us. Again, we were all up front for special prayer and as I walked back to my seat, she came behind me and, just like the day before, said, "God wants you to write a book about your stories." Once again I put it out of my mind.

That night I had a vivid dream and vision from the Lord. God was sitting at a table with His large hands laying flat down on the table. Then He picked up papers which were plain white with a blue edging around them. I could not see His body, but I felt His presence there. He said, "You can tell your stories about the furnace, the hospital and the others." Then He put the papers down and held His hands up and out towards me. As He did so, I felt His presence come towards me and He said very distinctly and emphatically, "I want the last chapter of your book to have the plan of salvation, the assurance of eternity in heaven."

That did it! That is my heart's desire here on earth to proclaim Jesus' salvation or being born again to be assured of one day entering heaven. I shouted, "Yes, yes, yes, I'll do it!." The thought of hell is so dreadful, scary, dark, and evil that you truly would not want your worst enemy to go there.

We do need to be qualified to go to heaven. The way is simple, but so profound. *John 3:16* is probably the most quoted verse from the Bible. I am realizing that God is a persistent God when He desires something. That is why I'm attempting to write this book. All the speakers at that seminar, including the Lake children, had books they had written. I checked over the book selection and purchased one from each speaker. At this conference, the authors autographed their products. I took the books home and from February until April, I never got a chance to look at them. Jill Austin's book had large handwriting by her name inside. It read, "Write the book, call it "Treasures of God" then she had put: "Storyteller-Visionary-Dream Big Dreams *Isaiah 58, Isaiah 62 and Psalms 91."* I loved reading those scriptures. Psalm 91 is my very favorite Psalm. I also loved the title "Treasure of God" so that is what I am using.

Due to Jill's requests, God's dream and the lovely note Jill had put in her book "Dancing with Destiny," I have a complete excitement now and desire to accomplish this. As I told the Lord, "You lead me and I will follow." He is in control, I am merely an instrument in His hands. In looking up Isaiah 58 that Jill had referenced in her note, God is preparing us to be mature in the Lord. Isaiah 62 is about seeing God's will be done and Israel be saved. I try to make Israel my daily prayer that our Lord save and protect Israel and the Jewish people.

Chapter 2
Jill Austin's Inspiration

Chapter 2
Jill Austin's Inspiration

Jill Austin, a prophet, speaker and teacher, passed God's message on to me to write this book. Jill Austin was President and Founder of Master Potters Ministries.

Jill's best Friend was the Holy Spirit. He filled the lonely places of her soul. The Holy Spirit was always with her. The Holy Spirit was Jill's Confidant, Counselor, Strategist. His tender companionship and guidance always points to the glorious Son, Jesus Christ. Jill heard the Holy Spirit's prophetic words and He gave her glimpses into eternity. The Holy Spirit is an intimate Friend. Jill embraced God's full purpose for her life.

Just two years ago, I was in the hospital's emergency room just waiting to be released. I was so lonely and anxious to be released to return home. I said, "Holy Spirit, I know You are here with me. Let me feel Your breath on my cheek." Suddenly, I felt a gentle, sweet breeze blow through my hair, face, and neck. It was so exciting and sweet. I was laughing and tears tumbled from my eyes in gratitude. I felt so blessed.

Jill Austin said the Holy Spirit can be meek or wild. He can be as meek as a gentle dove or as a roaring wind and consuming fire. He is not afraid of controversy. Our Holy

Spirit has a great love and wisdom. He challenges people to run for their highest callings. He gave Jill amazing grace. Our God is our Creator, a God of purpose and design. Always beginning with the end in mind. God declares the end from the beginning (Isaiah 46:10).

One of Jill's desires when she was alive was to awaken people's hearts to dream, love, and to war. Jill wanted us to have our minds transformed so we can see life through the heart of God instead of our circumstances. That our vision will be renewed and our heart ignited with fresh passion. Prophetess Jill embraced God's full purpose for her life. God directed her and gave her a special creative touch. In Jeremiah 29:11, God says that He knows the thoughts and plans He has for us; plans for peace and hope, not failure. "A journey with Jesus is exciting and fun," Jill used to say. God can do supernatural things with us.

Jill said Kathryn Kuhlman, a beautiful Evangelist, had dyslexia. She had to speak very slowly to get words out correctly. Jesus is eager to interact and fully engage with us in our daily life. We need to trust God. Jill Austin tells us to be a weapon to defeat the enemy and bring freedom to the hurting. With Jesus our potential is unrestricted. Jill tells us to embrace God's full purpose for our life to be a powerful weapon to defeat and bring freedom to a sick or hurting person. It seems the Holy Spirit will guide, direct, and give us the needed words when needed to deal with negativity that can plague us. Jesus says he weeps for the lost. He would be willing to be crucified and suffer again to bring the lost or negative people to salvation.

Psalm 139:13-16 says that God has planned a future for us before we were born. This does not mean that everything that occurs in our lives was pre-planned by God. God doesn't cause us to sin, to fail or experience devastation. It does mean He has a finish line in mind for us and a preordained way of recovery when needed. We are worshiping warriors, freedom fighters on a mission of mercy with God.

When God came to me in a vivid dream vision, He held up papers in his hands, white with a blue line around the edge. I am so grateful to my friend, Vickie Myers who typed ¾ of this book. As I continued to write more of the book, my very dear, capable daughter-in-law, Suzanne, took over the job. Suzy helped edit the book and add the new additions. I am so thankful to Vickie and Suzy for blessing me so abundantly.

God created us to be creative. Creativity will flow from us. God's Holy Spirit was placed in us when we received salvation. He brings new life to hearts open to His creative touch. The mystery of the glory of God comes out of His splendor and beauty to us. Don't let any negativity plague you. Words like, "I can't speak, not smart enough, I lack skills, am not a leader, I'm too old, so forgetful." Don't let any excuses and limitations disqualify you. I've tried them.

Jesus is eager to interact and be fully engaged with us in our daily life. Every journey has its ups and downs, difficulties, and sufferings. God loves each one of us so much. We are original, custom designed by God. He gives each one creative and dangerous assignments. Any negative actions invite the devil, who is always waiting for any moment he can interfere. Moments like this requires us to stop and put God's armor on and cover ourself with the healing blood of Jesus. God wants us to share His Words of wisdom to bless and encourage others with this security.

Chapter 3

From Generation to Generation

Chapter 3
From Generation to Generation

First, I will give you some of my background. I am one of seven children. Our father was Clarence and mother's name was Katherine. They met in school and started dating then. Mother and dad were married in 1914. All of my parents' families were ardent church members. My dad was the superintendent of Zion Reform Church (now called Zion Evangelical and Reform Church). He taught Sunday School each week in the large room that was packed with people. He could be found reading his Bible nightly at his desk. He and my mother never used curse words or showed fits of anger or told untruths. After they got married, they had three sons, Clarence, Daniel and Billy. I was the fourth child, their first daughter. I was a novelty for a while. Then another baby boy, Richard, came along. Later another girl, Katherine, was born. The last baby was a boy, Bobby. He was eight years younger than me. He was like my own living doll baby. I would rush home from school to care for Bobby. I would push him in my doll carriage and swing and sing to him for hours.

When I was in the 9th grade, I became aware of Ed Cochran when we were on the tennis team together. We played doubles together on the team and dated throughout high school. My best friends in our group, Mary and Bud, also fell in love and married after college. After my high school graduation, my family moved to Baltimore due to my father's business being there. He had worked for his dad, D. A. Stickell, who was in the mill business, then my dad became involved in imported foods, mainly sugars. Dad was also in the boating business and had several marinas. He taught navigation which was essential as World War II was taking place and boats could have been a way of escaping in case of bombardments.

I attended Mary Washington College in Fredericksburg, VA. Ed attended MIT in Boston, so we were separated pretty much for a while. Ed and I both had divine guidance and protection at every juncture of our lives. After marrying, we began our family two years later. Ed had a brother and I had five brothers so we were hoping for a girl. We had two boys then our girl. It was best that way because the boys were protective of their sister. We now have eight grandchildren, six girls and two boys. God does move in mysterious ways. At this time of life, I should have some great grandchildren, but so far only one grandchild is married. I am praying for a Mr. or Mrs. Right for my grandchildren for them to have a special marriage. This is one of my fervent prayers, *Lord, please send Christian spouses for my grandchildren; ones that will be Your selection. Help us to be patient until that happens.*

Now have your Bible by your side as you read this. I will quote or paraphrase scriptures and then relay incidents relating to His Word. We can be an earthly voice of God and be His hands by laying ours on needy people and walk where we are needed. In that respect, do His will, and He will lead you. Be a blessing for our Lord. This action is available for every person that desires and seeks His passion.

God speaks to us in a variety of ways:

1. His Word: II Tim 3:16 says that every word in the Bible is God breathed.

2. When we accept Jesus as our Savior, God places His Holy Spirit in us to guide and direct us. John 16:13 says the Holy Spirit will guide us into all truth. Holy Spirit is a person within us. As I need answers, I pray and ask the Holy Spirit to accommodate me, and He almost always answers.
3. The Lord speaks sometimes in our thoughts. Many times in church meetings and Aglow when we are seeking answers through prayer, most of us will get the same message or direction. We can't put God in a box. He does things differently and in new ways. God desires us to share our encounters with each other.

My Involvement in Aglow

I became involved with Women's Aglow, a Christian organization, in the late '70s. My neighbor, Dora, invited me to one of their meetings. Aglow is an international and interdenominational (all faiths) organization which holds meetings all over the USA and in 225 nations. Through Aglow, my eyes and heart were opened to a new revelation of the Holy Spirit. In my first meeting I attended, which was held at a local motel, the Venice Inn, I was rather cocky and informed the greeters that I was only there to observe. The room was literally packed to the point that many were standing. Most of them seemed so happy, but one lady near me was disheveled and distraught and went up front to be prayed for. She returned to her seat completely changed. She seemed to be peaceful and happy. God really hooked me that day. I thought waiting for the next meeting the following month was the longest month of my life. Needless to say, I have been an ardent attendee ever since. I received a completely new focus in life. I wanted to devour God's Word.

Another neighbor, Pam, became a teacher at a church, Zion Assembly of God, in Maugansville. I had remembered Pam as a really attractive, fun, party-type girl who smoked and enjoyed drinking. Then suddenly she was a Bible teacher! My curiosity at Pam's conversion got to me so I attended the class she taught at that church. What a marvelous change there was in her. She was a super Bible teacher. I caught her enthusiasm and have been attending that class ever since, even though Pam no longer teaches there. She was active in Aglow and was asked to be president of the local chapter.

Whenever an office needed to be filled, God always directed someone to fill it. The men also had an organization, called Men's Full Gospel and they met monthly at that same motel. Their organization was equivalent to our Women's Aglow, except wives and other women were invited to the men's meetings. They always had a special time for healing prayers. One night I was there and my arms were aching so badly that I went up front to be prayed for. As they prayed for me, they said "The Lord said to them to pray for my back to be straight." I thought they had really missed on that one, but I didn't say anything to them about it. Years later, several people remarked what a straight back I had. They would say that most people my age had slight curvatures or even humps. I told the Lord "Yes, God, I remember You had those men pray for me to have a straight back." My mother, her sister and both brothers all had curvatures. Praise the Lord! Thank You, Lord, for taking care of that way back in the 70's for me! My back is still straight to this day!

Through Women's Aglow, my relationship with the Lord grew. I never remember my family, who were faithful church members, or even the church we attended, emphasizing as the Aglow people did, that we must be "born again" to be able to enter the gates of heaven. My first office held in the organization was chairman of Bible studies. I had six Bible studies, great teachers and places to meet.

One day I received a notice if any of my teachers couldn't attend a class that I was expected to take over and teach. That really upset me. We had some dinner guests that night, but I went upstairs crying out to the Lord, *Why did You give me this position? You know I can't teach like the teachers I have!* I heard, *Maybe you can't, but I can. Trust Me.* We had an Aglow board meeting the next day and our president, Pam, said, "Is everybody content with their new office?" I stood up, weeping, "Please remove me from the office of Bible Study Chairman as I am not qualified." There was a pastor's wife there and she stood up and said "Jane, you have more active Bible studies than we have ever had before. Trust the Lord, He will provide." Fortunately, God is so good as I never had to fill in as a teacher, Praise the Lord!

God then made me secretary. I hated keeping notes and records, but with His help, I did well. To this day, I am an ardent note taker. The next position I was given was as treasurer. I thought that I can't even keep my own checkbook straight. I hung in there since I was handling other peoples' money, and became very conscientious and made it through that also. Consequently, I keep my own bank account in better order than ever which goes to show that God is in control and does provide.

Next, the Lord put me in as vice-president. I learned to do all kinds of obligations. I got the speakers, took care of their situations, sent our newsletters and monthly notices out. Then International Aglow Board had a new ruling that no one could be on an Aglow board more than eight years.

That saved me from having to be president. God is so good. I am still on the board, but with no particular job or office. Four of us had to leave our office due to that new ruling, since all of us had over eight years of service. Aglow did give me a new focus on life. The baptism of the Holy Spirit became vital. Jesus is the Baptizer of God's Holy Spirit. Jesus commanded His disciples not to leave Jerusalem, but wait for the gift His Father promised: the Baptism of the Holy Spirit (Acts 1:4,5). This gives you special power to be a witness for Christ, evidenced by a new language called "tongues," which is such a blessing. When you try to speak in your special language, your words sound like gibberish. That's what the enemy, the devil, wants you to think. Ignore those negative thoughts and say whatever the Lord gives you, which is unknown tongues, and continue to speak. The mystery words will increase and you will use and rely on your tongues gift.

Chapter 4
Filled with the Spirit

Chapter 4
Filled with the Spirit

When Ed and I were married and had our 3 children in the '50's, we joined Ed's church, St. John's Evangelical Lutheran Church in Hagerstown, where I am still a member and help my pastor by visiting the sick church members that are in nursing homes or hospital. I was visiting a member at Avalon Nursing Home whom I prayed for and gave communion to. The man said, "I want everything God has for me, even the special language." We prayed and his spiritual language flowed from him. We were both so happy. The man in the bed across from him opened his curtain that was around his bed and asked me to pray for him as I did for the first man. I was ready and so willing to do so. We prayed and he also received the language. We both laughed and praised the Lord. I emphasized to them that it wasn't me, it was God doing those miracles.

Back to the scriptures in Acts, Jesus went up to heaven forty days after His resurrection from the dead and then after ten more days, the Holy Spirit came on each of the ones waiting for Him. In Acts 1:8, Jesus told them He would give them power and in Acts 2:2-4 we see they were filled. Peter, one of Jesus' disciples, explained to the onlookers what had taken place (Acts 2:14-18). Luke 3:21,22 records that after John baptized

Jesus in water as Jesus was praying, the Holy Spirit in the form of a dove came on Him and a voice from heaven said, "This is My much loved Son, in whom I am well pleased." Jesus was thirty years of age and His ministry began after that event.

Continue with your spiritual language. It will flow out of you at times, such as when you have problems, see accidents, or when you are praying for someone for healing or to be cleansed from their sins. When we hold unforgiveness, we keep our Lord from being able to minister to and through us. We also keep the Lord from being able to forgive us as it says in Matt. 6:15. The Bible tells us that all of us have sinned (see Rom. 3:23 & 5:12), then Rom. 5:8 says Jesus Christ died for those sins, so we can be reconciled to God (Rom 5:10). A complete cleansing, What a relief it is and available to us all. With this gift of salvation, or being born again, we know that one day we will live in heaven with our Father, Jesus, angels and loved ones who will be there. That is so exciting to me!

This gift of salvation is the most important miracle in the world. Then to top it with the baptism of the Holy Spirit. Wow! (Ephesians 1:13,14 and Philippians 2:13).

I love the activities I am involved in at my local church, including the Wednesday night suppers and service, along with Aglow meetings and Zion Assembly Bible studies. I also belong to a Thursday afternoon prayer group and in all these, I feel blessed to be involved with our Lord and His Word. My children would put my name on any list of children's activities whenever there was a vacancy, which I was glad to do, unless it interfered with the dancing class at the Women's Club. My children would say "Why do you have to be there for that, mom?" I was on the Women's Club board for many years, even after being vice president. We had to help with every activity the club had. Back in those days, I helped to start the dancing classes for juniors and high school teens. My children all were involved. I spent much of my time at the Women's Club.

When our sons were interested in scouts, I became a den mother for them for quite a few years. I learned so much while keeping my scouts occupied. That's why I got involved in ceramics. I had my own kiln and worked with molding clay objects and we would make jewelry, pottery, etched metal trays, beading and painting. Just recently, one of my former scouts remarked about the wonderful gifts we made for their parents. It was a learning experience for me and I actually became a potter.

Meals on Wheels

For many years I delivered Meals on Wheels to sick people every week. I enjoyed visiting and taking prepared food to them. Oftentimes while I was there I would pray for them and talk with them for a while.

I was asked to take delinquent boys with me instead of them being sent to jail. I had several boys go with me, one at a time, for several months. I always prayed and asked the Lord to open the door so I could tell each one about the Lord. They seemed to love hearing about Jesus.

One time I turned the radio on as we were driving. Someone on the station mentioned God. The boy that was with me yelled, "Did you hear him! He said God, turn it up!" Of course I did. I only hope and pray that those boys still hunger for the Lord the rest of their lives.

I BEGAN TO PROPHESY

I was interested in almost every kind of craft. They came in handy for gifts. I knit for all the family and enjoy it. Just three years ago I was making scarves for my granddaughters. They were just plain, straight and narrow but I used unusual yarns. I decided I'd also crochet some scarves as they were very attractive. One of our local yarn stores advertised crocheting classes, so I took them up on it. I had a large ball of yarn but couldn't find the beginning loose thread. The instructor and two ladies in the class were actually pulling apart the ball searching for the end. I was standing and watching. I suddenly felt light headed and as I turned around to look for a chair, I fainted. I have never had that happen before. When I came to, I was lying on the floor with ambulance attendants all around me, giving me oxygen and taking all kinds of tests. I asked what I was doing on the floor when I just had come to crochet. A couple people standing there said a person was on each side of me and laid me on the floor. However, when I had turned to look for the chair, no one was behind me. I am sure God placed angels there to do that so I wouldn't be hurt.

I was informed that I had been unconscious for just three minutes. Then they put me in the ambulance and took me to the hospital. Ed, Jr. came to be with me. A doctor came and asked if I had ever fainted before. After a thorough examination, he casually remarked that he and his wife were being sent to Egypt by their church. He said he was worried about the trip. I sat right up and prophesied over him, saying, "Your trip will be safe, you will not have any problems, you will have angels around you." I assured him it would be a safe, fruitful trip. Rarely have I ever prophesied and at that moment, I didn't think that's what I was doing. The doctor then said he felt that God had this event happen to me so I could encounter him that day. It really didn't sink in until another doctor came and asked me the same questions as the previous one and as he was doing so, the first doctor reappeared and again said that God had that happen just for him. I thanked the Lord for using me, but requested that it might be in a gentler way in the future!

I was in the Emergency Room for quite some time with medical staff and people milling all about, but no one paying any attention to me. I would ask them when would I be able to leave, but a nurse finally came and said they thought it might be best if I would spend the night for more observation. I told her I didn't think that would be necessary and really wanted to go home. Finally, the nurse had me sign papers so I could be released. Ed, Jr. drove me to the yarn shop so I could get my car. I convinced him that I would be OK to drive. He led me in a round about way to my house so there would be less traffic to handle. I never had any more problems or reactions from that episode. I assume it was as the first doctor stated to me.

God cares about us. Praise the Lord! I just want to be useful to Him. My heart aches so much for the hurting people and I become bold and go right to our Lord on their behalf. After much consistent prayer regarding their sickness, troubles or whatever it is about, I release them and their problems to Him. Then it becomes God's problem as I pray for a positive outcome. I know God will or can change their situations.

One morning while driving to my Bible study, I said "Lord, You can use me today, I'm available." One of the ladies came to the meeting and told us she had been in bed several days with back trouble but felt compelled to attend the meeting. At this meeting, we go into the sanctuary of the church and worship the Lord for about an hour. I was in the pew behind that woman and prayed about her back. She was unable to stand when the rest of us did, and I sensed the Lord was telling me to lay my hands on her back. I kept gently rubbing her back as we were in the praise session. Suddenly, she jumped up screaming that her back was healed because all the pain was gone! She was in tears and so was I. Months later I saw her and she ran up to me with outstretched arms saying she was still pain free. Just recently she came to me and said "My back is still healed!" Thank You Lord!

Later, this same lady brought her son with her to the Bible study. He was a satan worshiper and came so he could try to change us to his way of life. Lois, our Bible teacher, prayed for him and two women there had what the Bible calls "words of knowledge" (I Cor. 12:8) for him. One of them said to him, "The Lord says you will be a godly man and will lead many to Christ." He had been holding papers with directions on them of how to turn us against God, but as he was prayed for, he began to crumple the papers into a small, tight ball, not even realizing he was doing so.

This story reminds me of one about the speaker, Pastor Werner, for an Aglow meeting. About nine years ago, I was planning on going with her church to Israel. Both she and her husband are pastors and they pray over who they should ask to go with them on those trips. The Lord gave her my name. Ed, my husband, and I had planned to go to Israel in 1996. However, he had leukemia and became so ill he wasn't able to make the trip and dear Ed passed away in May, 1997. When Ed and I planned a trip to Israel to visit the places where Jesus walked, we had our passports and vaccinations already. Ed awakened one morning several weeks before our trip and said, "I cannot make that trip." Ed never complained in spite of his having leukemia. He realized he was not able to make this trip, so, of course, we canceled it. Ed died a year later in 1997. We were praying for a miracle, but Ed went into a coma for two and a half days. The children and I were beside his bed at this time. We all prayed, "Lord we need a miracle, but if it is Ed's time to go to his heavenly home, we release him to You."

God's Word says that there is a time to be born and a time to die (Ecc. 3:2). Ed frequently said, "I'm not afraid to die and I'm not afraid to go to heaven but I'm afraid to leave Jane. Our middle son, Rob, said, "Dad, I'll take care of mother if the Lord wants to take you to heaven. Don't worry about mother." Pastor Heim came to see Ed at the time he was in the coma. The children and I walked into the living room so the Pastor could be with Ed alone. I heard the Pastor say in a firm voice, "Ed, it's alright. You can go with the Lord. Jane will be alright."

Ed died soon after that. I remembered Ezekiel's story when the Lord told Ezekiel he was going to die. Ezekiel pleaded for more time. The Lord gave him fifteen more years. During this time Ezekiel had another child. He was the worst child, very evil. I always felt I want to be ready when the Lord wanted me and the same for Ed and our family. I had a peace about Ed's death. We had fifty-three years of a wonderful marriage. I live in my precious memories daily. Time doesn't make it easier, but one day we will be together again. I'm enjoying my family down here and doing all I can to share salvation of Jesus with everyone so they will be accepted in heaven. That is my earthly mission.

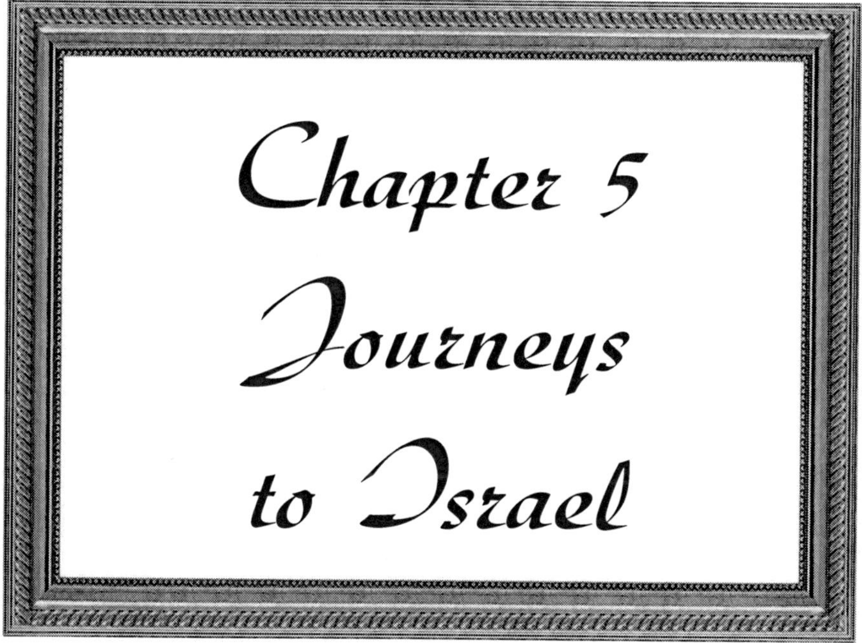

Chapter 5
Journeys to Israel

Chapter 5
Journeys to Israel

Pastor Werner called me about their church in Virginia going to Israel and asked if I wanted to join with them in 1998. She said they had room for some extra people, prayed about who should go, and the Lord gave her my name. When she called me, my spirit leaped within me and I had such great excitement. So I joined them. After we were all on the plane for the trip and waiting to take off, a lady across the aisle wouldn't buckle her seat belt. Several flight attendants tried to get her to do so without success. Then, the pilot came out and said he could not move the plane without everyone being strapped in. The woman said she would get off because she had been sick and couldn't stand to have the belt go across her. The airline staff all walked away, so I threw my arm across the aisle and told her to take my hand and she did. I prayed gently out loud for the Lord to calm her, give her inner peace and let her put the belt on. I also prayed for her to have a wonderful time and be able to enjoy the entire trip. In a few moments, the crew came back and she allowed them to belt her in. She laughed and enjoyed the whole trip. God really changed her, He is so good. Thank You Lord.

In Israel while walking over a bridge, one of the ladies in our group stopped and leaned over the wall of the bridge. I asked her what was wrong and she said she had a terrible pain in her chest. I reached over and laid my hands on her and prayed for God to remove the pain in the name of Jesus. She straightened up and marched up the hill over the bridge and actually led the walk. We praised and thanked God for being so good. Another day while there, we saw twelve gorgeous, handmade banners being held up and displayed in a parade. They depicted the twelve tribes of Israel. Suddenly, it began to rain. We prayed for the Lord to stop the rain so the banners, which were beautifully hand embroidered, would not be ruined. They were seven feet long and just as wide. As we prayed, the rain ceased until the parade ended, then it began again. Praise the Lord!

I have been able to go on three Israel trips with the Werners so far. Twice I was blessed to be baptized in the Jordan River where Jesus was baptized by John (Matt 3:13). Baptism is such a precious gift, such an immersion and cleansing. We were given long white robes to put over our bathing suits. Every person was prayed for so specially and lovingly. We were immersed completely. If some part of the body didn't go under the water, they would immerse him again. When it was my turn, I actually dove under the water to be sure I was completely swallowed up by it. I felt the Lord's cleansing, it was so beautiful and precious. The third time I was there in Israel, there was much unrest in that area so we didn't have any baptismal services.

Jane S. Cochran

While in Israel, we visited an Israeli Army Tank Base which was about fifteen miles from the Syrian border. The military force invited our group to have lunch with them. The boys seemed to be so young and friendly. They even wanted us to pray with them. We were shown slides of their maneuvers and tanks. The tanks were called Chariots of Fire and were exceptional pieces of equipment that God blessed them with. The soldiers demonstrated tank maneuvers and even fired them for us. As we stood in an open field, the tank shot out fire and huge smoke screens. The smoke screens camouflaged them from the enemy. The soldiers told us they would sing during training as well as combat. They also took us to the dry riverbed where David collected his five smooth stones, one of which he used in his slingshot to kill Goliath with (I Sam 17:40). I collected some stones there and still have them. I also have a picture where Moses sat in the special seat in the government forum. When we visited that place, I sat in Moses' seat too.

We all loved floating in the salt water of the Dead Sea. All we had to do was lay on the water and since it is so heavily laden with minerals, you would easily float. It was difficult to just stand up. If you got the saltwater in your eyes, it would burn and really be painful. People can float in that sea, but boats cannot. It would be hard for them to stay upright.

There aren't even any fish in the sea. That water has wonderful healing powers in it. The minerals in that water are valuable, and becoming more so all the time. Major health and beauty treatment centers and shops are all around the Dead Sea. The black mud from it is used to coat bodies for beauty treatment. The air there is special, desert dry, oxygen rich, pollen free, and no pollution. One day those minerals will be in great demand in the world. The hotels were lovely and had beautiful outdoor swimming pools. There were gorgeous flower arrangements to be seen too. Chapter 47 of Ezekiel, says the waters of the Dead Sea are healing and God is going to open it so the Mediterranean Sea will flow into it and fish will live in it. This will happen.

It seems as though each time I would plan an Israel trip, the devil would zap me with a bad problem. The third time before our trip, my right leg became paralyzed. My son, Rob, called an ambulance to take me to the hospital. There, I was told it was a strange case of arthritis. I had to spend three days in the hospital. I was able to take one of my granddaughters, Rebecca, on that last trip to Israel.

One night we spent at a camel farm. The next day there was a caravan trip planned on the camels. The owners had a two-person saddle on each animal. Becca climbed up and told me to ride with her. I told her I was afraid my leg might give out again, so she called the other ladies in our group to pray for me. Instantly the fear all disappeared and I felt I would be able to do it and got up on the saddle with some help. Becca turned around to face me and saw behind us a bunch of bowed heads in a circle and I knew they were praying for me. I was able to go the entire caravan with no trouble, and ended up not even sore or stiff. What a marvelous miracle!

While in Israel, a young couple, Christine and Peter, held healing services and invited Aglow to attend. The night before we went to their service, some boys came and began to heckle the family and cause a commotion. Peter invited the boys all to come up front on the stage with them. They went up, thinking they would really cause a ruckus. When on the stage, Christine and Peter asked them to form a circle and hold hands. Then the couple prayed in the Spirit. One of the boys was missing half his arm. As they were praying, God began to grow the arm out! It must have hurt, because the boy began to scream. Even a hand and then fingers formed. Everyone was in total shock. Needless to say, instead of heckling, they now all praised the Lord!

God does move in strange ways. More miracles happened in that seminar. A blind man's eyes were opened and healed with some type of matter running from them. A man who had a withered arm had a dream that Jesus touched him and when he woke up, his arm was healed. Another man had been in a coma forty days and he also had a dream of Jesus, who in the dream, spoke in tongues and the man's spirit understood the tongues. Jesus commanded the spirit of death to leave the man and it did. The man became conscience. Remember, Jesus said in John that if we believe (have faith) in Him, we can do what He did (John 14:12,13).

Don't tolerate sickness. Command it to leave in Jesus' name and be healed. It is always God's will for us to be healed. He says, "ask, believe and receive." Jesus' body was broken and bruised and received thirty-nine stripes for our healing. All manner of sickness, injury and death will fall in one of the thirty-nine stripes, accept it. The Lord tells us there is a time for us to be born and a time for us to die.

The Lord's Word is alive, active and will do what it says. Step out in faith. His Word will not return void. Ask for anything in Jesus' Name and He will heal you (John 14:13). His timing is always right. Healing can take even years for the process. God does allow us to have problems and sicknesses but He doesn't cause the situations. We actually benefit through problems. We become better equipped to meet the next problem and become stronger, more qualified. Remember when we are born again, Jesus' Spirit lives within us, and His blood delivers and cleanses us from the devil. The devil is just waiting every moment to enter through our sins and problems and cause havoc. This is a time to place the armor of God on (Eph. 6:10-17). You have authority over all the power of evil, the devil. Command the enemy to depart from you in the name of Jesus. The angels given us at salvation when we are born again will defend, protect and aid us. I'm going to share more angel stories later in the book.

Read your Bible and try having Christian music playing, especially worship music. A mail woman passed a certain house that always has worship music playing. She would stop, soak in the music and feel blessed. It happened around noon so she decided to bring her lunch, sit and eat it at that place. This mail woman said the affects of the music heightened her day. I find if I have a restless time trying to fall asleep, I'll turn on a CD of music and my mind stops rambling and I sleep.

I have heard that in heaven our spirits will understand all languages. Our spirit body is what goes to heaven when we leave the earth. It has the appearance as our earthly body. We will recognize loved ones. They will look as they did at the height of their vitality age on earth, in their 30's. I say that because the Lord took my spirit to heaven three years after my husband's passing so I could see that Ed was happy and well. He looked wonderful, so healthy and young, like he did when he was in his 30's. Ed always wore glasses on earth, but there he didn't have them. Since I had just asked the Lord to let me see Ed, I only saw things in heaven, I did not hear anything. I felt so elated seeing Ed being so happy in his heavenly home. When I visit the sick church members, those in the hospital or nursing homes, I am always so glad that Ed didn't have to be there. He had suffered and was in bed before passing onto heaven, but I know I will join him there one day and we will both be alive and well when the Lord is ready for me to go.

In Israel we took an "All Nation" prayer walk. They wore their native costumes and carried flags. We Americans wore red, white and blue and carried the Jerusalem flag. This walk went past strategic places like the Prime Minister's office and other Government buildings. The Jewish Israeli men had long curls on the sides of their face that reached their shoulders. They wore sawed off top hats. Children, mostly boys, were dressed in suits and hats like their dads.

The Dome of the Rock in the middle of Jerusalem had a beautiful golden top. The outline of it remains the same since the year 691 even though it has been repaired many times.

We went to the desert mountains where the Dead Sea Scrolls were found. To get to the area, you can go by desert jeeps, camels, or even on foot. The scrolls were discovered in 1947 by a Bedouin boy who was searching for his lost goat. The cave entrances in the cliffs are very pronounced, but difficult to get to. The scrolls were placed there 2000 years ago in clay pots since they have been dated as being from 520 B.C. There are eleven caves. Many copies of the Old Testament of the Bible had fragment copies hidden there. Now they are housed in the storerooms of Rockefeller Museum in Jerusalem behind protective glass. The handwritten copy of Isaiah chapter one in the original Hebrew language was wrapped in linen covered with black wax and sealed in earthenware jars. The most remarkable find was the immense library of the manuscripts in cave four at Qumran. Every single book of our Old Testament is there except for the one of Esther. Traveling in Israel, the streets are extremely busy. Many traffic jams, but no accidents, horn blowing, police or sirens. It seemed to give you a peace. I felt the presence of God and had an awesome feeling of security.

The empty tomb where Jesus had been laid was so impressive and sacred. We all wept being in there. The pillow Jesus' head was on was a large, smooth stone. The huge round stone that had covered the tomb entrance and rolled away by the angel was there (Matt. 28:2). The gardens up in front of the cave were beautiful, so vivid. I could really feel the presence of our Lord. It permeated the surroundings. Our group took Communion there at the tomb. The hill behind it was high and part of the cliff had crumbled and formed what looked like a skull. Over the tomb entrance was a sign that read, "He is not here for He has risen." Joseph had asked Pilate for Jesus' body and his request was granted (Matt. 27:57-60). Joseph wrapped Jesus in a clean linen cloth and placed Him in his own unused tomb. Both peace and sadness were felt by us being there.

Olive trees that are 1,000 years old are located close by. Their trunks are huge but the branches are small. Jesus spent nights under these trees praying since it wasn't safe for Him in Jerusalem. We took a boat trip on the Sea of Galilee just as Jesus did. The seagulls were flying around as we threw bagel pieces into the air so they could retrieve them. It was a peaceful and nostalgic trip. All of us in our group wept.

My heart does yearn for Jerusalem. Pray for God's Jewish people. God's new name for Jerusalem is City of God's Delight and the Bride of God. In spite of unrest there, I felt such a peace and that God does rejoice over us as a bridegroom rejoices over His bride.

Chapter 6
The Greatest Weapons

Chapter 6
The Greatest Weapons

Prayer

Psalm 138:7 says, "Though we are surrounded by troubles, God will bring us safely through them." The Lord will work out His plans for our life. Read Psalm 139 and be blessed. God will lead you along the path of everlasting life.

One of our greatest weapons is prayer. Pray for peace in Jerusalem often, daily. When peace takes over in Jerusalem, then peace will be in the world. Prayer is a divine weapon. It can destroy enemies, forces of darkness, all fear and courage is gained. Nothing is impossible with our God. Those martyred on earth have a special crown in heaven. God's greatest prophets, Elijah, Jeremiah and Daniel were persecuted. They remained faithful and are rewarded in heaven where there is no persecution. Stephen asked God to forgive those that killed him. Saul, who later became Paul, being one of them, was completely turned around and is responsible for most of the New Testament, as we read in Acts 7:59,60.

Grace

Another great weapon is grace. The grace of God is amazing. Grace came through Jesus. Jesus is the fullness and grace of God and puts the indwelling presence of God inside us. We are all in need of God's grace. His grace saves us. Romans 5:1-2 says, "Therefore, since we have been justified through faith, we have peace with God through our Lord Jesus Christ, through whom we have gained access by faith into this grace in which we now stand." Grace is opposite of self confidence, it takes our eyes off ourselves. Grace of God is stepping out of self consciousness. The enemy tries to get us into self-consciousness. Grace gives us finite created beings intimate contact with the loving God. We get healed with God's power when we are in His grace and all the fullness of God is available to us.

Grace is generosity. We try to help others receive God's grace. It is better to give than it is to receive. God desires to take what is in Him and put into us. Charity of God is the fruit of the Spirit. Compare God's freedom with frustration, insecurity, pressure, self-pity and doubts. God's grace will set us free. Experience the everlasting presence of God. Pray as the psalmist did, "Search me, oh God, You know my heart, test me, You know my anxious thoughts. See if there is any offensive way in me. Lead me in the way everlasting" (Psalms 139:23). *Lord, if there is anything in me that makes You sad, point it out to me. Lead me along Your path of everlasting life.* We are to offer unconditional grace as Jesus does.

The grace of Christ precedes our mistakes and our grace must precede mistakes of others. Our love should not be doubted. To have a heart like Jesus is to touch grimy parts of people and repay their unkindness with kindness. Eph. 4:32 says, "Be kind and compassionate to one another, forgiving each other, just as in Christ God forgave you." When conflict occurs, forgive by using grace, and move on. People are thirsty for mercy.

Jesus compares our ears to soil; hard soil, rocky soil, a weed patch overgrown, too thorny. Some have good, fertile soil, but probably about 75% of us miss messages and don't use our ears to really hear. Spend time with God. Listen to His voice. Jesus often went to lonely places to pray and to be alone with His Father God. So we need to clear our calendars and pray. Luke 4: 4,8,12: Make time with God, it will be the highlight of your day. Open the Bible, He speaks to us through His Word, the Bible. Holy Spirit helps us to remember as John 14:26 states.

Pray first, read the Bible prayerfully, meditate on the scriptures. Search the Word like hunting for silver or hidden treasure (Ps. 1-2). Choose depth over quantity. Write it down, study over and over, just as when we were children and first learning (Prov. 2:4,5). Matt. 18 talks about us becoming childlike, not childish. Have a listening ear and apply the changes to your life. It will bring greater glory to be changed to be like Jesus (II Cor. 3:18, Philippians 4:9). God tells us to listen to Jesus As God softens your heart, be hungry, willing and expecting.

As we become more like Him, our face can reflect His goodness. We can reflect the glory of the Lord and as His Spirit works within us, we become more and more like Him (II Cor. 3:18). God can change our faces, wrinkles of worry can disappear, shame and doubt can become portraits of grace and trust. God relaxes clenched jaws and smooths furrowed brows, bags of exhaustion are removed and tears of despair turn into tears of joy and peace. Our faces change through worship. God is in the business of changing the face of the world with a prepared and willing heart.

When I have prayed for people, I have seen their countenance change as God penetrates and heals them. Just recently I was at Sam's Club in the checkout line. There was a couple behind me. The wife was being verbally berated by her husband. She walked away from the line over to the exit door and waited for him there. He took her purse over to her and returned back to our line. I found myself saying to him that I saw him do that and it was so nice of him to take her purse to her. I told him how lucky he was to have his wife as I lost my dear husband and miss him so much. I felt God had put those words in my mouth, because I had been thinking how nasty he was to her. I wanted to berate him.

As I was putting my purchases in my car, that man walked up to me and said, "Thank you for talking to me." His whole countenance was different. I think what I had said, God's words really, had made him ashamed and know how fortunate he was. I doubt if he deserved the kind words, but he needed to hear them.

Fasting

Fasting cleanses and heals. Many people are healed by fasting. It detoxifies our body. I've heard that many wise people fast one day each week. I don't and haven't done that. It surely would help one from gaining weight. When I feel I should fast as directed by the Lord, it is always a benefit. I receive an inner peace and yet an encouragement. It still amazes me when I declare a fast that hunger always leaves me. Thank you, Lord.

We must also not talk "poor health." Prov. 18:21 says that death and life are in the power of the tongue. Our words can be a blessing or a curse. What we believe and speak affects our body, including our immune system.

In Luke 6:45, Jesus said that a good man out of the good treasures of his heart brings forth good things and an evil man brings forth evil things, for out of the abundance of our hearts, the mouth speaks. James 3:2-11 explains what an important role our words play. And Prov. 18:7 goes so far as to say that a fool's mouth is his destruction and his lips are the snare of his soul. Mark 11:24 says, "Therefore I tell you, whatever you ask for in prayer, believe that you have received it, and it will be yours." The devil gives sickness, as he is the one who robs, kills and destroys (John 10:10) but God's will is to heal. Jesus redeems our life from destruction.

Persistence overcomes failures. You will have resistance, but as the Lord says, Don't give up when you make mistakes. Quitters never win and winners never quit. Wounds equip you for leadership. Reject sickness. Never question God's promises. His Word never fails. Ex. 15:26 says He is the Lord that heals us.

Fear

Problems are the storms of life and are inevitable. During the difficult times we don't have to let our lives be in a turmoil. Read II Tim 1:7, "For God did not give us a spirit of timidity, but a spirit of power, of love and of self-discipline." The Lord tells us not to fear because He is with us. Fear is the opposite of faith.

When we find ourselves in a situation where fear is trying to set in, the first thing the believer should do is pray, putting the situation into God's hands. When someone does something bad to us, our first human instinct may be to get back at them in some way, this is fear trying to work. Faith does not retaliate when wronged, but believes that God will work and protect.

God has plans for us to prosper, not harm us, to give us hope and a future (Jer. 29:1-13). He wants us to call upon Him and pray to Him and He will listen to us.

He tells us to seek Him and we will find Him. Get lost in God's presence, you have much to gain. Don't feel as if you are bothering God either. We are so highly favored by Him (see Ps. 8:5).

Jer. 33:3, "Call to Me and I will answer you and tell you great and unsearchable things you do not know."

One time I joined my husband on a trip to Baltimore. He had special business appointments, one right after another. I decided to do some shopping and left the stores so I would be on time to get him. The location where I was to pick him up was in an area that was unfamiliar to me. I couldn't find the street and found myself circling around many times and was in tears. Finally, after much frustration, I prayed. I looked up and right there in front of me was the designated street sign. I truly felt the Lord translated me to the right place. I made it just in time. Praise the Lord!

Fear causes us to rely on our own strength. It is the opposite of faith. When weary, go to Jesus. Stress cripples. Don't feel sorry for yourself. Use every problem as a learning experience. We can learn obedience through suffering, problems and illness. Be strong, and your battles can bring you to promotion.

Ps. 139:14 tells us that we are fearfully and wonderfully made. We are each one of a kind, an original design and unique. We now know our fingerprints, hand and footprints are all specific unto us, along with even our set of genes.

Speaking of fear, one night I had a vivid dream that Ed was lying dead down by the furnace. When I awoke,

I rebuked that vision and commanded it never to take place. I plead the healing blood of Jesus to wipe it from my memory. It never happened, thank the Lord. That vision and those scary thoughts left me too.

Here is another treasure story: One evening the furnace suddenly made a huge noise. It was frightening and I ran to the phone to call the man who takes care of that equipment for me, but there was no answer. I remembered Ed had some different people work on the furnace before, so I got a name from my phone book. A man named Jack came right out and told me that he had done work on our furnace previously, but he hadn't heard from me for a while. Then I remembered that we did have a furnace man who had admired Ed's miniature train set in the basement. A few days after he had been there, we discovered three very special trains were missing. No one else had been in the basement. I stayed with Jack for a while as he worked on the furnace, but then went upstairs for a short time.

When I returned to the basement, I didn't see Jack. I called for him, but he didn't answer. I thought he had left and as I started up the stairs to see if his truck was still there, he suddenly asked if I wanted him. I knew he was checking out things in the other room. My son, Rob, called just then and I told him the circumstances and he said to stay with Jack as he might need something. I grabbed a box of old papers that I wanted to dispose of to check through them again and sat on the cellar steps. I told the Lord that Jack needed to know Him so he would stop stealing and to please help me here. Still sitting there, I asked Jack if he was married, he said he was divorced. After a while, I asked if he had children and he said no. I asked the Lord to tell me what I should say next. It came to me to ask him if he belonged to a church. He replied a sharp "No." In slight agony, I said, "Jack, if you died, and we all have to take that trip, do you know where you would go, would it be heaven or hell?" He said that any place would be better than where he was in his life now. I told him that isn't so because heaven is wonderful and I told him a little about it. Hell is dreadful, being so evil, dark, no fresh air to breathe and you burn in a lake of fire forever and ever. Again, I asked the Lord to tell me what to say next. I looked down at the box of papers and on the top was a booklet titled "Heaven or Hell." I never saw that before. I picked it up with tears streaming down my face. Jack then wanted to show me what he had done so I went down the rest of the steps holding onto the booklet.

After I saw how he fixed the furnace, I told him I had a booklet about Heaven or Hell. I asked him if he would read it. He literally grabbed it from me and I felt the Lord had prepared his heart.

He left, and months, maybe even half a year passed, and I needed the furnace worked on again, so I called Jack. He said in a gentle and kind voice that he would be happy to come over. He looked very different when he arrived, as there seemed to be a sweetness about his character now. When I asked him how he was, he said he was great, that his life was wonderful and that he met a lady he wanted to marry. He then thanked me for what I had done that previous night. I told him that I had never seen that booklet in that box of papers before and know that God had made that for him just at that time. I even told him I would like to read it myself, but he said he didn't know where it was. God and I sure were smiling.

Chapter 7
Overcoming

Chapter 7
Overcoming

John 15:16 says God chose us. He gives us free will which is the power to choose, to make decisions and we have the ability to turn from sin to Him. He takes our every sin, forgives, cleanses and never even remembers our sins again (see Ps. 103:12). Romans 10:9,10 shows us how to get our passport to heaven. Jesus came to earth, gave His life by shedding His blood to remove all our sins. Rom. 3:23 tells us that we all have sinned. Sin is what keeps us from God. It is against God. The wages of sin is death, as seen in Rom. 6:23. Through suffering and problems we can learn that His timing is always perfect, even though at the time, it may seem to be slow. He is never late. The fear of the Lord, as spoken of in Prov. 8:13, is respect and reverence of God and Jesus so that we hate evil and everything that is against them.

Matt. 6:14,15 & 18:35 says we must forgive others. We must not only forgive for the other person's sake, but for our sake. If not, it can cause disease and will warp our hearts and bodies. Long ago God taught me about forgiveness, how it increases the more it is used. The devil is always waiting for an entrance to us and to get us to make mistakes or do wrong things. Women usually are more tenderhearted and give in and are more gullible. Eve ate the forbidden fruit first.

Romans 12:2 says we need to be transformed by the renewing of our minds, then we will be able to test and approve what God's will is. We read in Romans 8:6-8 that the mind of the sinful man is hostile to God and brings death since it does not submit to God's law, nor can it do so. Those such minded cannot please God. The mind controlled by the Spirit is life and peace. Philippians 4:8 tells us how to renew our minds and think on what is true, noble, right, pure, lovely, admirable, excellent and praiseworthy. John 8:32 says know the truth and it will make us free. God gives us ability to move on after failures and rejection. Remember, God has no favorites. We are all awesome in His sight.

Also remember the enemy, satan who is the devil and the evil one, is always trying to interfere by giving us negative thoughts. He is always waiting for his moment to influence us. Greater is Jesus in us than he who is the devil that is in the world (1 John 4:4). The devil can be recognized by his rude entrances, interferences and words.

God has given us an armor to wear for the battle. Eph. 6:10 tells us to put it on daily and the enemy won't touch us. I always try to spiritually place the helmet of salvation on my head because it protects completely the head: mind, eyes, ears and mouth. Put on a shield or breastplate of righteousness around your chest, the upper body, where our heart, lungs and inner body are so they are protected. Gird your waist with the belt of truth. Shod your feet with boots of peace. We need peace. Lift your hands to cover your body with the shield of faith. I envision covering my life, house, yard, car, and family so this shield of protection will keep the enemy away. Trust it. Do it. In your right hand you have a two-edged sword, God's Word, which is so powerful that it will cut loose anything the enemy tries to put on you.

God wants us to be fruitful and multiply so we can spread His good news. His sweetness, kindness, love, hope and encouragement renews our spirit. Never put yourself down because Jesus and God's Holy Spirit are in you. Put a smile on your face! God made us from soil to red, yellow, and brown; then blew His breath into us, so I think that's why we are white, black, and yellow. Remember, God uses the foolish things of the world to confound the wise (I Cor. 1:27). Our spiritual bodies in heaven will all be glorious and shiny.

Romans 8:15-17 tells us we do not receive a spirit of bondage. We are God's children, so we are heirs, and co-heirs with Christ. II Tim 1:7-9 says God has not given us a spirit of fear but a spirit of power, of love, and of a sound mind. God wants to save us and call us to a holy life through His grace. Believe and trust in the Lord and your Holy Spirit. Don't speak fear, instead speak faith.

A personal treasure example of this is when I was walking down a darkened alley toward my car. A man was coming really forcefully towards me and I prayed for the Lord to protect, help, and cover me with His blood. Suddenly, the man became frightened, stopped and straightened up and slid along the alley wall to get away from me. I'm sure God placed an angel beside me. Angels can be huge and seen by the people God wants them to see. Do warfare like II Cor. 10:4,5 says. "Our weapons are not carnal, but mighty in God for pulling down strongholds, casting down arguments and everything that exalts itself against the knowledge of God."

James 4:7 tells us to submit to God, resist the devil and he will flee from us. Be strong and know who you are in Christ Jesus. "Greater is Christ that is in me than he (devil) who is in the world" (I John 4:4). John 10:10 tells us the thief (devil) comes to steal, kill and destroy, but Jesus comes to give life and life everlasting. Call on the name of Jesus, cover yourself with the protecting blood of Jesus and you will be protected and blessed. Remember, Jesus shed His blood and received thirty-nine lashes, called stripes in the Bible, and then went to the cross to protect and heal us. There is a stripe to cover every sickness or injury.

In II Timothy 2:26 we read about the enemy enslaving people to do his will. In Luke 4:18, Jesus said He will set those captives free from the power of the enemy over them. Some of the ways we are held captive by the enemy are becoming broken, bruised, oppressed, greedy, addicted to things like alcohol, cigarettes and drugs, gambling, lust, sexual desires and adultery. Jesus Christ sets us free from the law of sin and death and breaks the devil's bondage on us as we see in Rom. 7:21-25 through 8:2.

Acts 10:38 lets us know that God anointed Jesus with His Holy Spirit and power so He could do much good by healing those who were under the control of the devil and in the spirit of bondage. Read Rom. 8:13-17 so you will know about freedom. Repent, ask forgiveness and you will be restored with peace, joy and love. *Abba Father, accept and restore me.*

Read Ps. 23:4. Trust that God's Word will do what Isaiah 55:11 says. It will not return void. Halleluiah! John 14:12 tells us that if we believe, we can do what Jesus did and even more. Wow!

Storms of life are inevitable, but during the storms, we don't have to let our lives be in turmoil. Mark 4:36-39 tells of the time Jesus and His disciples were in a boat in a storm, being tossed about. Jesus had fallen asleep while the disciples were fearful and afraid. Jesus had no fear. His disciples should have trusted being with Jesus. Jesus' words "Do not fear, I am with you always" in Matt 28:20 are reassuring, even when we walk through valleys of death, we are to fear no evil because He is with us. My daughter and her family experienced an earthquake and felt the house move. She was screaming and her four year old daughter, Lindsay, said "Mommy, don't be afraid, Jesus is with us." Storms of life do come. Don't lose your focus from the Lord. Many times we allow circumstances to become so great that we do lose our focus on the Lord. We don't fail until we fail to get up.

Stress is a personality that cripples and causes spiritual infirmities. It can make us ill, have pain and depression. Migraines can be a spirit. Cast it out. A lady named Marylyn had migraines for fifty years. It was cast out from her and she had none after that. Breathe out stress, command the spirit of stress to leave you. Shake your hands and neck and command it to leave. Command worry and fear to leave. Be loosed and be set free in Jesus' name. Boldly command in Jesus' name that the roots of stress will leave you now and never return.

Lord, let Your peace and rest come in. Lord, You take over, let Your love, peace and joy come in. You can believe that the Lord wants to set you free. Read Ps. 149 (out loud if possible). Praise the Lord because praises of God will bind the enemy. Stress, hate, rebellion, depression, jealousy, anger, strife and suicide are problems that can be cast out and away from us. Luke 4:18 lets us know that Jesus fulfilled what was written years before in Isaiah 42:6-7 to open eyes, set you free, and be released and He has already won the victory over all of the above. Is. 61:1-3 foretells of Jesus, who would preach the good news and proclaim release of captives to set them free. If evil man turns from his sin and does what is right and just, he will surely live. His sins will not be remembered. Mental depression can be guilt buried so deep, you have forgotten it.

Generational curses can flow from fourth generation and even back further. You don't have to keep curses, pray, and ask God to break curses and restore you to normalcy in Jesus' name. A blessing can be passed on to a thousand generations. Souls need to be transformed and set free, hearts need cleansing.

Just recently, I was talking to a beautiful Christian man, Les., whom the doctor said had a blood clot in his esophagus and must be removed right away or it could take his life. He said that he didn't accept that diagnosis and didn't believe it. He told the doctor to give him a week and if it was still there, then he could operate. When the day came, the clot wasn't there! All the doctors came in to double check and they were completely confused. I hope they realize what a wonderful God we have, that when we ask and believe, we receive.

Father, don't let one person that reads this leave today without accepting Your miracle gift of being born again. Born again is the most valuable, important gift. This is our passport to heaven. Please remove any negativity, unforgiveness, anger, resentment, failures; anything not of You, Lord. Cleanse each one completely in Jesus' name. Thank You. Help them feel Your wondrous love and lead a life that honors You. A new person will come forth.

The Israelites spent forty years in the wilderness because of lack of faith when they could have been out in eleven days, several weeks, much sooner. Don't let our hearts turn from You.

Help us to love our spouse and be a helpmate and look for the good in them and in our children and friends. Help us be the person You desire us to be, a designer's original. As we go through trials, You, Lord Jesus, walk through them with us. You never forsake us. We can grow through our trials. Help us to be more like You, a child of God. I pray this in Your precious name, Jesus Christ.

Spend hours in prayer and fasting, waiting on God, which will come easy when God is in control (Matt. 17:21). Jesus said you can do nothing of yourself (John 5:19,30). I find in everything I do, I need His help and I get it when I pray to Father God in Jesus' name. Our Holy Spirit gives us power, see Luke 24:49 and Acts 1:8.

In II Cor. 4:16, God reminded me not to lose heart, though outwardly I am wasting away, yet inwardly, I am being renewed daily. For our light and momentary troubles are achieving for us an eternal glory that by far outweighs them all. Set your eyes not on what is seen, but what is unseen, for what is seen is temporary, but what is unseen is eternal.

A couple years ago in September, I was taking a walk in the late afternoon. I was up past the third hole of the golf course at Fountain Head. All of a sudden, my right hand was pulled so hard that it turned my body around towards the direction I was leaving. It was so sudden and strong, I temporarily lost my balance. I asked the Lord why He did that as I hurriedly retraced my steps. I heard the words, *Harm's way*. I thanked the Lord as I proceeded as fast as possible. I then asked Him what was harmful. A boy was going door to door so I asked if he was the cause of the harm, but I heard, *No.* I asked if a truck was coming? No again. Then I asked if a golf ball was coming my way and I heard, *Yes.* The rough is very narrow there, so a ball could easily come into the street where I had been. The Lord told me, *There were four golfers getting ready to drive their balls off the tee"* I thanked the Lord for protecting me with tears of joy as I hurried back down the road.

"So do not fear, for I am with you; do not be dismayed, for I am your God. I will strengthen you and help you; I will uphold you with my righteous right hand" (Is. 41:10). "To fear the LORD is to hate evil; I hate pride and arrogance, evil behavior and perverse speech." (Prov. 8:13).

When I asked the Lord that I wish I could see my husband in heaven, I prayed that Ed doesn't appear to me with no expression and just lift his hand casually to me. I actually had that vision; that he was expressionless, grayish, and lifted a hand casually in a wave to me. I felt a sickening disappointment. Then I said "That is not you, Ed." I said very emphatically to get out of here now and the vision disappeared.

The next night my spirit was in heaven and I was sitting in what looked like a box car. Ed appeared at the opening, which was a large open door. He had the biggest smile on his face, his hands outstretched and looking very young and handsome as he had been in his 30's. He always wore glasses but he didn't have them on. The Lord revealed to me that He took my spirit to heaven. It was such a beautiful, exciting and loving experience. It blessed me so. The devil delights in filling us with doubts, especially God's word and His goodness. We have authority over the devil, so use it.

God isn't behind terrible calamities, sickness, big problems and mistakes. As I am writing this, treasures of

God examples keep coming to me. We have a stone wall around our driveway. At one place there is an opening. Two steep stones make the steps but we have nothing to hold on to. Whenever I go up or down this area, I always ask the Lord to hold my hand and help me get over this wall and I am always able to do it without a problem. A while ago, I hurriedly went down the steps and at the same time was talking to the neighbor and I neglected to ask the Lord for help. I fell and landed halfway in the garden and the stone wall. I cut my leg and arm. Just because of one moment of neglect. When people often have accidents or sicknesses, they blame God. Don't blame Him for your calamities. It can be carelessness on our part.

We need to have strong faith as well as believing in God. Believe in God, that He exists, and that He can deliver healing and settle problems.

I misplaced or lost my driver's license card for almost two weeks. I searched my car, house and pocketbooks, but no license. I mentioned to my hairdresser that I couldn't find the card and asked if she found it in her shop. She said no. The lady having her hair done next to me told me how serious that can be and you can be charged big bucks if police stop you and you don't have your license. Another lady said they can even arrest you and put you in jail. When I got home, I asked the Lord to please help me find the license. Then, I thought that maybe I should get another one that afternoon, but I heard the Spirit say, *No.* I felt this was alright and that I would wait until the next day. The next day I talked about getting a new license, but again heard, *No.* I thought, *Lord, why don't You want me to get a new license?* Then I wondered if He didn't want me to drive that day.

Again, I waited another day and got another no answer from Him. I said, *Lord, You must know where the card is, so we are going to the sofa and please tell me where it is.* As we reached the sofa, I asked Him to come and tell me. I asked the Holy Spirit if it was in the car, or in the kitchen where I would make exchanges from a coat pocket to a pocketbook? Each time the Spirit said no. Then I asked, *Is it in a pocketbook?* Finally the answer was yes! I had checked my pocketbooks, but maybe it had slipped into a lining of one. I rushed up the stairs and again searched very carefully. No license. Then I saw a small, dressy bag that I remembered using just once lately. I picked it up and knew immediately that it was in there. I praised and thanked Him with laughter and tears of joy.

If you have fears about something, admit your fears. Believe you can have what you desire by asking and believing for it. Turn to God, and trust Him for the answer, healing or whatever it is you want. Then pray and believe and you will receive. God is not afraid and we who believe in Him should not be fearful. If you have God's Spirit in you, then you have the part that is necessary. The Spirit controls all things, even fear. When Jesus and His disciples were in a boat on the Sea of Galilee, a sudden storm arose and frightened the disciples and they called to Jesus to help them. Fear developed among them. Jesus spoke to the storm and it ceased (Matt. 8:23-27).

I can remember several times we were having picnics and it started to rain. I commanded the storm to cease in Jesus' name and the storm stopped. It would begin again after the party. God is so good.

When I was in Israel, my group took a boat trip on the Sea of Galilee. The weather was lovely and seagulls were flying all around us. The boat captain had a supply of bread crumbs and we threw them out and the gulls would catch them in the air. I thought about the boat trip Jesus and His disciples had taken. I felt blessed because all was calm and lovely for us.

In Matt 8:5-10, we read the account of the centurion who entered Capernaum and went to Jesus and told Him that his servant was at home lying sick of the palsy and was very ill. Jesus told the man He would go and heal him at his house, but the centurion told Jesus that He only had to speak of healing his servant and he knew he would be healed without even going to the house. The Roman centurion explained to Jesus that he had authority and when he gave orders, he had soldiers who obeyed them. Jesus marveled at the man's great faith. So Jesus told him that as he had believed, it would be done for him. Sure enough, when the man got back to his house, the other servants told him that the sick man got well and it was at the time he and Jesus had discussed the situation. This shows how powerful faith is. Ask, believe and receive. That centurion was a Roman army captain stationed in Capernaum when Jesus was there. He had heard Jesus speaking and saw healings that He did and must have even spoken to the people. He saw Jesus as the Healer, Miracle Worker, and Preacher of deliverance.

We Christians that read our Bibles and see all the miracles and blessings that Jesus did should also have strong faith and expect to see miracles. We should be against sin, disease, fear and demons. Jesus healed by the touch of His hand and His word and said in John 14:12 that if we just believe and have faith, we could expect to do what He had done and even greater things. Jesus told us to speak the word and expect results. Healing for our body is more closely connected with our soul. Healing is more than physical, more than mental, it is spiritual. It involves an act of your soul.

The saving of our soul is the greatest miracle in the world. We must believe Jesus Christ of Nazareth is the Lord and believe in Him as our personal Savior. Believing Jesus to be your Savior will affect and change our mind and heart. It will give us a new set of values, a new way of life and great peace. Good doctors, medicines, nature, understanding and love can all aid in healing. James 5:15 says the prayer of faith shall heal the sick. Points of contact are important as we see in Matt 9:20,21 when the woman touched the hem of Jesus' garment and the laying on of hands from Acts 8:17 which is one instance where the Holy Spirit entered and power was transferred. The woman made Jesus' robe her point of contact. It wasn't the robe that healed, it was her faith in that point of contact. When she released her faith, Jesus released His power. I felt the same point of contact presence when I picked up the bag that had my driver's license in it, as I just knew the card was in it.

My left knee had a dislocation problem in it. I prayed to the Lord for Him to put my knee in place and told Him that I would appreciate it. Then I could concentrate on the arthritis there. Two days later I was listening to Pat Robertson on the 700 Club and he said in a word of knowledge from the Lord, that a lady's knee needed to be readjusted and the Lord was doing that. At just that moment, I felt a movement and a change in that knee. Praise the Lord! I did not have to have my knee operated on. Faith has complete mastery over every disease. If someone lays hands on you, believe and feel like it is Jesus' hands. Think only positive thoughts even through pain. You'll win healing.

Speaking of faith, this summer I cut my leg on a long nail that was put in a socket to hold a huge wheel in place on a cart. The cut was a good four inches long and almost a half inch deep. It bled profusely, so badly that I couldn't leave the garage to even make a call for help. With much pressure and rags on it, I finally made it to the kitchen and called one of my sons. He drove me to the medical facility, but they were so busy that I ended up waiting almost two hours to be taken care of. I was able to stop the bleeding by then. They didn't want to stitch it as I am on a blood thinner, so they meticulously taped it together.

Five days later, our family was all getting together to go to the beach. I had been baking, cooking and packing and didn't really have any time to think about my leg. I took the tape off when I had been told to but it wasn't healed yet. The wound was still red with a deep indentation from the cart. I tried to make an appointment with my regular doctor, but his phone line was constantly busy. My leg looked so bad, I was afraid I would be put in the hospital. At this same time, a well known evangelist was at a local church. I thought if I went to the meeting, I could get him to pray for me for healing of the wound. I drove out to the church and slipped in to sit in the back as the service had already begun. I was only there about an hour, when the evangelist's wife got a word of knowledge from the Lord and said, "There is a woman here that came for a healing on her leg and God wants to heal it." She even said that the lady's name is Jane and pointed to where I was seated!

Such a miracle. I was desperate and went up to them and they prayed for my leg to be healed. As I was walking back to my seat, the evangelist's wife also said that there is someone here who feels neglected by the Lord and not being used as she would like to be. I said that's me also and turned around and returned for more prayer. The pain in my leg subsided and when I looked at the cut, it wasn't as red and open as it had been. When it was time for the family to leave for the beach, my leg looked much better. My leg healed a lot while at the beach, but since it wasn't completely healed, I didn't want to get in the pool or ocean. There is a large scar on my leg, but I am beyond worrying about scars. God really did a miracle on me, as I know only He could have healed it.

The key to healing is believing. Faith has complete mastery over all diseases. As I believe, I will be healed. Great faith recognizes Jesus' power over sicknesses and diseases. Believe and don't give up so you will get results. As one's faith increases, God's power in their life increases. Cultivate your faith and it will grow stronger.

Think positive thoughts about life. In times of discouragement or loneliness or confusion read the Bible. Luke 10:19 talks about the power Jesus has given us, which is all power over the enemy. This says nothing shall by any means hurt us. If the enemy is bothering you, read Luke 9:54-55 and you will see that Jesus came to save people and not destroy them. Sickness, oppression and fear are not sent to us by God, but by the devil, so command him to leave. Jesus says in John 10:10 "The thief comes to steal, kill, and destroy, but I have come that they might have life and have it more abundantly."

Philippians 4:19 is a good scripture if you need money: God supplies all our needs according to His riches in glory by Christ Jesus. Ps 23:1 and Psalms 37 & 91 are good if you need strength and confidence. Matt 8 for healing, Mark 9:23 tells us that if we can just believe, all things are possible to those who believe.

Chapter 8
Cursing and Blessing

Chapter 8
Cursing and Blessing

Curses

When bad things happen, or when we are disobedient, we open the door to the enemy, the devil, to come in. He works constantly to get you out of balance.

John 10:10 tells us the thief comes to steal, to kill, and to destroy; but Jesus said He came to give life everlasting, and to the full extent.

Jesus laid His life down for us, only to take it up again-see John 10:18. He gives us eternal life, guaranteeing us a place in heaven, where we will never die again, be sick, lost or perish. No one can snatch us from the Lord (John 10:28).

Deut. 28:15 says that along with the promises of God spoken through Moses, came the assurance of cursing for disobedience. But curses will come if we do not obey the Lord. If we do not obey His commandments and statutes with which I charge you this day, curses will come upon you and overtake you (Deut 28:15-19). The Lord curses the enemy and the devil is always waiting for us to lie, cheat, or sin in some way that opens the door for him to have access to us. He will try to convince us that wrong can be right. But Jesus keeps us in perfect peace when our minds are on Him.

Ed and I were skiing one weekend during the cold winter season. We loved to ski, and had learned how when Ed was stationed in Reno, NV during the war. We had just gotten married a few months before going to Reno. This particular occasion, we were in Pittsburgh skiing and stayed in a hotel for a couple of days. Ed, after being in our room a short time, became ill. That was very unusual for him. We called for a doctor through room service. A foreign man came who was very hard to understand since his English was limited. There was a flu going around the area at that time so I asked the doctor if Ed had the Hong Kong flu? He asked if we had just come from Hong Kong, and we laughed, and he gave Ed some medicine and left the room. I sensed a strangeness in our room and the thought came to do spiritual warfare. I bound every evil spirit, sickness and occult with the cleansing blood of Jesus and Ed's sickness left him.

We learned from that experience to do a spiritual cleansing every time we would spend the night in a hotel or motel. We traveled frequently so it was beneficial to know to do that. We would command every spirit to leave the rooms in Jesus' name. I meticulously, spiritually covered entire rooms with His blood. All kinds of evil spirits can be in hotels or motels due to the vast numbers of people who use them. Some symptoms from evil spirits can be nausea, headaches, bad dreams or nightmares and insomnia. One can also have behavior problems such as arguing, restlessness and no peace. Some people even see ghosts, objects moving by themselves, foul odors, atmospheric heaviness and difficulty breathing. Just remember you have authority over what the enemy tries to place on you, so use it!

One April I had an inflamed lump below my breast on my right side. When this lump had appeared, my doctor put me on antibiotics. He felt it should be lanced but since I had an artificial aortic heart valve, he didn't want to operate near that area. Finally, it cleared up, but then it came back again. I immediately gave it to the Lord and praised my Father for removing it and thanked Him for allowing it to never return. In the meantime, I was scheduled to see a new doctor, an oriental woman. She was going to operate the day after my prayer. I was on the operating table, ready for the surgery. She felt for the lump, but could not find it. I, somewhat apologetically, told her that I had prayed for my Lord to heal it and said He must have done that. That doctor seemed to be agitated and told me she had another patient waiting and left the room. I dressed then left. I was elated, but feeling a little guilty. She ended up charging me for the operation, which I gladly paid for. At least I got to plant a seed in her, hopefully.

Cancer is a physical sickness that can be a curse with a spiritual cause brought on by the devil. When cancer is a spiritual cancer, it is caused by demons with what the Bible calls fiery darts (Eph. 6:16), or can be from generational curses. Greed, lust, pride, hate, anger, violence, or any of these can bring on spiritual cancer. We have the authority to break family curses in Jesus' name.

Much earlier in this writing, I had told about a lady who had brought her satan worshiping son to our Bible study. His mom told us that for Halloween he had dressed as Jesus. He looked perfect for the part, as he had long hair, was slender, tall and handsome. He is married and his wife and children are born again believers because of the influence of his mother. But there was a demonic curse on that family. His mother's mother was a satan worshiper and his mom had been also until she converted to Christianity. The curse has now been broken, Halleluiah! God does move in mysterious ways.

To have the baptism of the Holy Spirit gives one a more powerful ability for prayer and healing. When you become born again, God places His Holy Spirit in you. Forgiveness is so essential in receiving miracles. When we become angry over situations, even if it is not our fault, holding unforgiveness, we are going to cut off all sources of benefits from the Lord. The Bible clearly tells us that we must forgive or our Heavenly Father will not forgive us (Matt 6:14,15). Even if you have a right to the anger, do not hold unforgiveness. Pray in the Spirit. God has a way of diminishing the problem. Ask Jesus' help in releasing hurts so you can forgive in prayer.

Please forgive or more and more troubles will come forth. I learned early in my Christian walk the value of forgiveness. I received inner peace when I forgave. If you don't forgive, a turmoil builds up and can even get out of proportion or control. When we choose to forgive people, it releases God to bring miracles in our lives.

All of heaven rejoices and magnifies God when miracles take place. You have angels when you are born again, even though you can't see them. They record all miracles in detail that go into the Book of Life kept in heaven. Even the exact time you became born again into God's kingdom. If we don't obey God's commandments (Deut. 28:15) the devil enters. This causes havoc and curses come and overtake us, causing confusion, depression, accident proneness, marriages to fail, and suicide. Command curses to leave in Jesus' name. You have that authority by being born again. Revoke curses, drive out demons, cover yourself with the protecting blood of Jesus (Deut. 28:15-68).

In the name of Jesus, I release myself from Gal. 5:20 from any evil inheritances. I break the curse in the name of Jesus. Cease now and leave me and never return in Jesus' name.

Inheritance sins can keep attacking families for many generations. They will cause problems for many generations, but they can be broken. Command them to cease and leave in Jesus' name. Witchcraft is a curse when one manipulates or dominates as seen in I Sam. 15:23. Rebellion is as bad as the sin of witchcraft. Stubbornness is as bad as worshiping idols. Read Galatians 5:19-26 and 6:1-10, they will be so enlightening. If we don't honor our parents, we lack blessings from God's favor. Don't speak negatives, not even in jest, it can cause curses to come.

God embraces us in our weaknesses. Our mistakes are covered by God. Thank God for we learn through our weaknesses and Him, do what He desires. When we are weak, God can make us strong. Our spirit and our angels won't allow you to go in porn shops, betting places, gambling casinos or bars.

I learned to smoke when I went away to college. It seemed at that time that everyone smoked. Ed had to teach himself to smoke a pipe. When we would entertain, almost every guest would be smoking. I used to have ash trays on every table. Thirty years ago after returning home from the beach with my family, and having smoked excessively while there, my throat ached so much. I had tried to stop the habit many times but wasn't successful. When I walked into our kitchen, I stopped and prayed, "Lord, please remove this desire of smoking from me now. I thank You and praise You for doing this, in Jesus' name." I kid you not, from that moment, I never smoked or desired to smoke. Even the smell of cigarettes didn't entice me. God is so good. Thank You, Lord.

Speaking of smoking, I feel this is a curse. My son Rob's secretary was very ill in the hospital. She was a continual smoker. She was so ill, she was going to have to quit her job. Her heart and lungs were very bad. I went to the hospital to pray with Sally. As I entered her room, she asked if I would have my friends pray that she would stop smoking and have the desire removed. I told her that I was going to do that right then. We prayed for the habit to cease and the curse to be gone and never return. We prayed for our precious Lord to restore her health and remove all sickness in Jesus' name. Then, we thanked Him and praised Him for accomplishing this. My son, Rob, called me later that evening so excited. Sally was a new person and the desire to smoke was completely gone. Her lungs were functioning normally. She was going to leave the hospital and return to work. That was a huge miracle, and our God can accomplish anything.

If you desire to help people and are truly born again and have the baptism of the Holy Spirit, be bold and pray for the sufferer and God will use you. He said for us to ask, believe and we will receive. The baptism of the Holy Spirit gives you boldness and effectiveness. John 14:12,13 says that we can even do greater miracles than Jesus did while He was on the earth, because He went to heaven to be with God. You can ask anything in Jesus' name and He will do it. It will bring praise to the Father because of what Jesus does for us. In John 14:14, Jesus said we can ask anything in His name and He will do it. That is powerful, so believe, trust and take Him at His word. Don't be afraid to keep asking the Lord for the things you need. Then in verse 15 He says that if we love Him, we will obey Him. Verse 16 says He will give us another Comforter to be with us forever, the

Holy Spirit. He will never leave us and will lead us into all truth. Just think, Jesus lives in you and the powerful Holy Spirit is also there, never to leave. You are so blessed and anointed. The Holy Spirit will teach you much.

Jesus gives us the keys of the kingdom of heaven we read in Matt. 16:19. That tells us that whatever we bind on earth will be bound in heaven, such as my personal example of smoking and losing the desire. Whatever is loosed on earth is loosed in heaven. The baptism of the Holy Spirit allows us to win victories over the devil.

You need the baptism of the Holy Spirit (Acts 1-5). Here are some things you can do to break curses in your own life or others. First, pray in the name of Jesus (Eph. 5:20). Give thanks for everything to God, the Father in the name of our Lord, Jesus Christ. Command all the bad spirits to leave and rebuke these powers in Jesus Christ's name. Then loose the person being oppressed in Jesus name. Rom. 12:1,2 lets us know that our souls have three parts, and all three parts must be controlled by the Spirit of God to be in harmony with God and ourselves:

1. Intellect. This must be renewed after salvation.
2. Emotions. We need to control emotions. (Read Gal. 5:20-21.)
3. Will. Our will must be yielded to God's will.

If you are tormented by bad thoughts and deeds after repentance, you need deliverance. If you have a spirit of fear (like Job), a curse, sin, disobedience, uncontrolled emotions or occult connections and practices, then there are gaps in your hedge of defense.

Curses, which can be negative words spoken against one, can cause sickness. Uncontrolled gossip can cause backaches, unexplained tiredness and can be caused by negative words. So, choose your words wisely. For instance, don't ever say to someone, "You give me a headache," as such a negative remark can bring that to pass. Some more examples are, "I wish you were never born", "You will always be poor", or "You will never amount to anything." Such words spoken in a fit of anger or frustration that, unless the power of those spoken words are broken, can set a path of a person's life. In Jesus' name, you can be set completely free. Such good news! God's word will not return to Him void as it says in Is. 55:11. His word accomplishes things.

A mother called her child a "child of satan" and that child became involved in deep sin. Break those curses by praying in Jesus' name for healing and change. God does answer those prayers, so use His power and pray and wage war against the enemy. Bind and cast out and make those words null and void and of no power in the name of Jesus. Ask forgiveness for ever saying such things and you will be forgiven.

Witchcraft can operate in churches if a pastor allows manipulation such as bought favors. Just recently I heard this story. A mother was pregnant with a little girl. The mother was having difficulty during the delivery. Her husband was upset over his wife's discomfort and said out loud, "I hate little girls!" and hit his wife's stomach. The little girl was born and she had a strange fear of her father. Whenever he came near his daughter, she would turn away from him and cry. This went on until she was old enough to talk. Her dad said, "Why do you always turn away from me?" She said in a loud voice, "You hate little girls!" Babies can hear, understand, and can be terrorized by harsh negative words, even in the womb.

On the other side, A pregnant mother always sang a special song to her baby in the womb and patted her stomach. After that child was born and old enough to sing, that little girl would often sing the song her mother sang to her when she was in her stomach. Jesus Christ can deliver us from bondages and oppressions (Ps. 139:24). Pray: *Oh God, if there be any wicked way in me, lead me in the path of everlasting life.*

Sin opens the door to curses. Bloodline curses can be inherited such as fear. Physical conditions like heart trouble, migraine headaches and diabetes, to name a few, can all be caused by generational curses. Abused children often grow up to become abusers. Inherited addictions, and things such as lust, being unwanted and rejection can come down the family line. Here are some scriptures showing what type of curses can come because of disobedience or sin:

1. Curses resulting from abortions or oppression of helpless widows and orphans. (Deut. 27:18,19, 20-23,25).
2. Disrespect of parents will shorten your life (Eph. 6:2,3).
3. Respect and pray for Israel. Countries against Israel are against God and many are now deserts, such as Ethiopia. Love the Jewish people. (John 4:22/Acts 13:47).
4. Don't take communion flippantly (I Cor. 11:27-30).

Jesus has the power to break all bondages. After receiving the baptism of the Holy Spirit, recognize evil spirits in people. Do warfare and deliverance on their behalf. Follow Matt. 18:18 and 12:29 by first binding the strong man (the powers that hold people captive) and then loosing the oppressed person, in the name of Jesus, from the chains that are binding them. Demons carry bad words and accuse us as we read in Rev. 12:10. Listen to healing scriptures, 100 times if you have to, until they sink in. Claim and do what it says in Prov. 4:20-22 where it tells us to attend to God's words, by inclining our ears to listen, our eyes to see and keep His words in our hearts. They are life to those who do and health to our bodies.

There was a woman who was deformed. She was unable to walk or talk, due to a spastic tongue. Her mother read, believed, and prayed the scriptures for over fourteen years. One day, she was healed in an instant.

Go to God and trust His word. Enter into a covenant with Him. Don't say, "If it is God's will" because He made it clear in His word that He wants us healed and whole. It is always His will and He can do divine surgery.

Use your prayer language for creative miracles. Get healing for your family. You have authority, especially if you are the head of the household.

A son, Daniel, had a club foot. His dad, who was a doctor, claimed a perfect foot for his son. Now, Daniel is not only healed, but he is the fastest runner in his school.

If the problem is a strange growth, speak to its roots to dry up. Command that to happen in Jesus' name. Continue to believe and don't doubt. Speak positively.

A baby had Down's Syndrome and his parents prayed for an hour in their prayer language. They spoke healing words over him until he was healed. Don't panic, speak God's Word. His Word will not return to Him void. Faith is never in a panic.

Jane S. Cochran

A child was in an accident and dying. By faith his mother repeated the scripture "he will live and not die" (Ps. 118:17) probably 100 times. He lived!

Jesus desires to bless us far beyond our expectations. We are self centered, preoccupied and self willed. We can keep God at a distance. Anger, critical pouting, silent treatment and threatening are not God's way. We cannot keep peace if we indulge in negatives. God can change our attitudes, personalities, strengths, and our righteousness. He can set our souls free (Ps. 51:10). Trust Him. Actually, brokenness in us can make us better. Just like a rose, when it's crushed, releases its fragrance.

When we are hurting, have trials and suffering, God can redevelop us. John 15:16 tells us God chose us to bear fruit in His name. We need to trust Him. He desires to bless us. Allow Holy Spirit to lead you. Walk in faithfulness. God does have plans for you. Let Him perfect them in you.

One time I felt so bad that I was moaning. I heard Holy Spirit say to me that if anyone else felt that way when I was near them, I would lay hands on them and pray for their healing. I gave that sickness to the Lord, thanked, praised Him and I felt much better.

In Jer. 29:11-13 the Lord says He knows the plans He has for us. Plans to prosper and not harm us. Plans for a hope and a future. He tells us to call on Him and pray to Him and He will listen to us. If we seek Him with all our heart, He promises us that we will find Him.

Chapter 9
Prophecies

Chapter 9
Prophecies

I was very hesitant about including this in my book. The thought came to me though, God has no favorites and what He has done for me, He can do for others.

Back in 1995 at an Aglow Outreach meeting, a lady named Linda, gave a public word of knowledge to me. The Lord said through her that I have a heart of compassion. I feel what others feel. He was bringing me into a place where I would see beyond my eyes. He was stirring the gifts within me, to feel things and see beyond what people are saying and what they are appearing to be. He has given me a heart of love. I would be able to minister to people. I am to step out in holy boldness and not to worry about being offensive. God was taking care of that because of my heart.

Another woman, Fran, also associated with Women's Aglow, travels east every spring from California and prophesies to people across the USA on her journey. Fran said the Lord told her I was faithful and I allowed and prayed for Him to direct me. I do pray for guidance daily and do as I feel He leads me. I ask for direction and correction. He taught me to forgive early in my life. No matter what, I cannot hold any unforgiveness. God asked me to teach my family and all my grandchildren the value of forgiveness. Matt. 18:35 is the end of a story about how our Heavenly Father would treat us if we don't forgive others from our heart. God said that by my forgiveness, I have set myself free and not only that, I have set others free as well. Then He can deal with me, my family and others. God wants us to share the gifts we have learned (Is. 59:21).

Every Thursday I go to a church for prayer and Bible study. I have been attending that study for about 25 years. We always go into the sanctuary first to sing and praise the Lord. As we praise and worship God, I envision opening a curtain and entering where God and Jesus are sitting. I used to ask God if I could sit on His lap. I envision laying my head on His chest. Now I just enter and sit on His lap. Usually tears run down my face. Tears of joy and gratitude. I always take tissues into those praise times as I can't keep the tears back. I have never told anyone about these incidents.

One time Fran came as usual to this area and prophesied over me at a friend's house, which is where she usually stays on her visit here. Fran will close her eyes, pray in the Spirit and listen as God reveals messages to her about the person before her. As she prayed over me, she remarked that God wants me to know He loves it when I sit on His lap. I was totally shocked. As I said, I never had mentioned those episodes to anyone for fear they would think I had lost it. But now since He spoke about it, I feel free to tell others. It is confirmation for me. That just goes to show that God knows everything we do. Even simple things. He is so awesome and precious.

I am always praying for guidance and answers to decisions I need to make. I will pray in the Spirit and wait until I get an answer. Sometimes when I pray for an answer, I can get a quick, rude, abrupt or sharp answer. I then know immediately that was from the enemy, the devil, who is interfering. I stop and command him to leave immediately. I then pray in the Spirit and cover myself with the blood of Jesus and then I get a sweet answer from my Lord. Rarely, do I not get an answer.

Back in September 2001, I was in Frederick at Cornerstone Church to hear a prophet, James Goll. A friend signed me up to receive a prophecy and Jim Goll was the one who prophesied over me. Jim told me that God said I was faithful and God was being faithful to me. God told Jim to tell me that He wants to bless me for blessing Him. Within my own heart, the Lord wants to extend an extra measure of comfort to me. The Lord said through him that I felt at my age I was not able to be used anymore and that was absolutely not true. He wanted to bring me into remembrance of Abraham and his age, Noah and his age, and all the ones that God used at the ripeness of their age. God said the fruit picked at its ripeness is the best tasting. God wanted to extend His comfort to me in a revelation way, so I will continue to walk in the fullness He has called me to.

God can always see some good in each of us and our actions. He said my ministry is not done. Another prophetess named Amy, also at Cornerstone Church, prayed over me & through her, God showed her broken pieces of glass at my feet. He told her that signified that where I have been broken, He is picking up the pieces and putting them back together again. Also, that He is setting me free to do what He has called me to do. He is going to use me more than I have ever dreamed of and it will not be a long time down the road and will be in the near future. God wants to encourage me as He is going to bless me more in ministering and touching people. He wants to raise a creativity in me, and that I have some already, but He wants to enhance it and strengthen me even in writing, such as creative journaling. Amen! Do I need that. This is a prophecy about my writing a book in 2008. I had forgotten that God had said that. My writing a book was the farthest thing I would have thought I could do.

The prophetess I spoke about earlier, Fran, prophesied over me again that God has a reward for me laid up in heaven. God said He wants me to rejoice when I think of heaven. I do.

Fran also said she sees God giving me new truth, so I am to speak it out, especially to people my age. He said many are stuck in their religion of long ago. Fran thanked the Lord that I will proclaim what He is to me today and that I will set people free from religious spirits and the bondage of religion and into the true freedom of the gospel. Fran laid her hands on me and thanked the Lord for health and strength for me. She also prayed that if there is anything attacking my body in any way, for Him to send resurrection power in Jesus' name to every cell and for them to come alive in the Lord. Anything that is not of You, Lord, we just flush it out of her body and bring new life and strength to her body in Jesus' name. Don't let contamination of their spirits affect me. Help me to be wise and aware of problems (Jude 20-24).

Mr. Trout at a local church prophesied over me that God isn't through with me yet. My work is not done. God made a covenant with me that all my children and my grandchildren and their families will walk with the Lord. None will be lost. Wow!

I'm believing that and still waiting. Even the rebellious ones will come to the Lord, he said. I pray their beliefs and actions will be heart knowledge, not just head knowledge. It is easy for us to say we believe, but never to bring our thoughts and prayers out of our head knowledge to our heart knowledge. That is when Jesus really takes over and deep peace, love and a joy surrounds us and is in us. I'm praying, believing, trusting, rebuking and delivering towards that end. God wants us to be fruitful.

I want to mention that every time I have had a prophecy, the prophet always makes a CD of the message and gives it to me. It would be so difficult to keep their prayers and messages complete otherwise. I have listened to them many times.

Chapter 10
Hell

Chapter 10
Hell

Hell is a real place. The Bible teaches it both in the Old and New Testament. Everyone whose name is not written in the Lamb's Book of Life will be thrown into the lake of fire (Rev. 20:15).

In Luke 13:3, Jesus warned that unless one repents of sin they will perish. Paul said the wages of sin is death. A rich man dying is going to hell because he rejected God. He could see those who had rejected Christ as Savior. He sees satan who persuaded them to reject Christ. There was constant torment and pain that will last forever and ever as there is no medication to cure it. You'll hear crying and moaning of those suffering. You will beg for cool water and there will be none. No fresh air, only darkness and pain and suffering. There is no rest day or night only weeping, wailing and gnashing of teeth (Matthew 13:42).

There is no hope of ever escaping hell. Remember God had to destroy a whole world of ungodly people with a vast flood. Later He turned the cities of Sodom and Gomorrah into heaps of ashes then swept them into the face of the earth. He saved Lot out of Sodom because Lot was a good man. God knows how to rescue godly people from trials even while punishing the wicked, the proud and arrogant. False teachers, liars, those following lustful desires and those that despise authority will not make heaven. Now those suffering will remember the pleadings of parents, pastors, and friends to accept Christ. Memory and regret will torture them forever.

Those who indulge in sexual sins, idol worshippers, adulterers, thieves, greedy people, drunkards, abusers and swindlers, none of these will have a share in God's kingdom (1 Cor. 6:9-10). But your sins can be washed away and you can be set apart for God. Jesus Christ made you right with God by giving His life on the cross and now your name can be entered in the Book of Life. If you ask and believe in your heart that Jesus is Lord and ask Jesus to forgive you of all your sins. Satan is the one who blinds the eyes and ears of unbelievers so they are unable to hear the Christian's good news and they won't be able to see the glorious light of the Lord that is shining upon the Christians.

Our adversary, the devil, is as a roaring lion that walks about seeking whom he can devour (1 Peter 5:8). He comes to steal, kill and destroy. When evil spirits are within us, they cause us to quarrel, fight and rebel (James 4:2). Battling desires within us cause us to fight and rebel. You want something but don't get it. Some kill and covet but don't get it. You do not have because you did not ask God for help. I find even the simplest things that go wrong are righted as I go up in prayer. Just the day before yesterday, I had a weird hurting pain suddenly in my head, like nothing I ever had before. I thought this is of the devil then I got bold and attacked the enemy. I commanded the pain to leave and never return to me now in Jesus' name. The pain ceased and has never returned.

We need to deal with the enemy, as David did with Goliath. Goliath being so huge, so strong, so evil, no one would fight him. David, a godly boy was encouraged by the Lord, picked up a stone and with his sling shot hit Goliath with one stone and killed him. I'm sure our God guided that stone. (You can read the whole story of David defeating Goliath in 1 Samuel 17.)

Philippians 4:6-7 tells us to be anxious for nothing but pray and God's peace will guard your heart and mind. The Armor of God Eph 6:10 says, "Finally, be strong in the Lord and in his mighty power. Put on the full armor of God so that you can take your stand against the devil's schemes."

When you first try to speak in tongues (as it is called) you might just get a single word. You'll dismiss it as nothing important. Hang onto it. Use that one or 2 words. It will grow into a special private language for you. The devil doesn't want you to have this special language called tongues. The devil can't understand this language. Tongues is worth having and very beneficial. The devil hates the name of Jesus and especially the blood of Jesus which is a protection. If I feel a need for protection, I cover myself spiritually with the blood of Jesus. If I hear a strange noise in the house, the devil will even cause sounds to unnerve you. I just yell out. I don't have any fear, but get bold and angry and speak out against the devil. It works. "My house is covered by the blood of Jesus." Sounds cease. You will recognize your spiritual language because words are often the same even though you don't know what they mean. I have always heard we are praising our Lord and being blessed and protected when we speak our spiritual language. I love praying in tongues. It comforts me.

God does move in mysterious ways. Philippians 4:6-7 tells us not to worry about anything, but pray about everything. Let your requests be made known to God and the peace of God will keep your hearts and minds through Jesus Christ. Fix your thoughts on what is true and honorable and right and think about things that are pure, lovely, admirable, and about things that are excellent, worthy of praise, and the God of peace will be with you. Have positive thoughts as negative thoughts only bring trouble. Negatives are inner anger, unforgiveness, unbelief, and not trusting. God gives us power over the enemy (Luke 10:19). Prayer offered in faith makes the sick well and the Lord raises them up and forgives all sins (James 5:15). Don't only rejoice just because evil spirits obey you; rejoice because your name is registered in the Book of Life as a citizen of heaven (Luke 10:20).

Ed, my husband, and I were in Washington attending a dinner and a business meeting. We couldn't find any place close to the building where we could park that wasn't completely full. So we had to park blocks away and it was evening so we took a cab. The cab driver turned on his radio and it wouldn't work. He moaned and groaned over that and complained how everything had gone wrong. When we arrived at the hotel, Ed got out of the cab to get his wallet out of his pocket to pay his bill. I leaned over the back seat and stretched my hand out over his hand. I said I just want you to know "God loves you so very much. You are very special to God." I then got out of the cab and Ed reached in to pay his fare. The cab driver said to Ed, "I just want you to know this day has been the worst day in my life. Your wife has made it the best day of my life." Just think what a little prayer can do for someone.

Prayer is so powerful. It is like quietly opening a door and slipping into the presence of God. There is the stillness He listens to our cries. Then we can hear His thoughts or voice and receive His healing. Sometimes you might need to repeat the prayer until results come. Don't give up!

Several years ago I had a cataract operation. I had no fear as many friends have had this ten minute operation. My doctor said my cataract had completely broken up into small pieces and he wouldn't give me any medication or anesthesia because he needed me to be alert to help him remove each segment of the cataract. Oh how I prayed. The pain was dreadful. I was grabbing the sheets and mattress afraid I'd have them in shreds. It took almost an hour and a half, not ten minutes! I was completely exhausted. The doctor and nurse both said it was amazing how I came through it. He said it was one of the worst cataract operations he ever had. I said, "Oh, I was praying constantly. The Lord got me through it." The doctor said, "Oh, I was praying also."

I was totally blind in that eye for ten days. I belong to a prayer group that meets weekly. Rich, the leader, called me and prayed with me on the eleventh day. After Rich's prayer, I got a pinpoint of light in the corner of my eye. Then the next day, Pastor Heim, came out and prayed for me. That pinpoint started to gradually spread until finally I could see normally. I have a slight heaviness in that eye and my good eye has a patina, a creamy background, where the healed eye has a distinct white background. But that doesn't bother me at all. I'm just so utterly grateful for the miracle. Thank you my Lord for this miracle.

Luke 16:19-31 says hell is the final separation from God (which is the worst of horrors). The Bible also says that it is better to lose a hand or foot if they cause you to sin. Cut it off and throw it away. Better to enter life maimed or crippled than have two feet or two hands and be thrown into eternal fire. If your eye causes you to sin, gouge it out, throw it away. Better to enter life with one eye than be thrown into the fire of hell (Matthew 18:7-9).

We are told in many place in scripture that Hell is complete darkness, and that it is a place of great sorrow (Matt. 8:12, 13:42,50, 22:13, 24:51, 25:30, Luke 13:28, Mark 9:43) There the fire never goes out (Rev. 20:10). Those who are in hell will be tormented day and night forever (Rev. 20:15). Anyone whose name is not in the Book of Life or is not born again, will be thrown into the lake of fire (hell).

Repent because the kingdom of heaven is near!

Pray this prayer: *Father God, help me to forgive no matter what comes against me. Help me to draw near to you. Holy Spirit, thank You for living in me. Help me always to do the right thing and Jesus, thank You for your living in me. Thank You Father in Jesus Name. Jesus, You gave Your life to cleanse me from every sin and forgiveness. Thank you and guide me always. Please forgive me from all my sins and help me to always forgive no matter what.*

The Bible says that all in heaven rejoice when a person makes the decision to let Jesus be their Lord. The Book of Life is huge, and our name is in it. As we conquer problems, they are then miraculously erased and replaced by the good. We don't escape life, we overcome life. The Bible tells us we are more than conquerors through Christ Jesus (Rom. 8:37). God can keep us waiting for His glory for a purpose.

Jane S. Cochran

One Christmas holiday, an Aglow friend had taken a homeless woman into her home. I fixed Christmas gifts for the woman and took them to my friend's house, which was outside of Hagerstown. Leaving my car motor running, I got out and retrieved the presents from my back seat, shut the back door, then leaned against the front door which caused it to close and lock. I went inside and called my husband, Ed, and told him of my predicament. He came to her house and unlocked my door for me. Dear Ed, he never found fault with me, just cared and was so helpful. After visiting the house guest, I left to go home. I drove up a hill, and not being able to see on the other side, I encountered a large truck just in front of me. There was no place to pull onto the side of the road. I shouted a prayer and I looked, and all of a sudden, the truck was behind me! I was in such shock that I stopped. It had to be one of God's miracles. It seemed so bizarre that I didn't tell anyone about it for a long time. For a moment, I was scared to death.

The enemy loves when we talk about death, so we need to watch what we say. As a Christian, we should not talk about being scared to death. Find a different way to express what you are saying. Words are powerful, and the enemy may try to make your words factual. I am learning to conquer this.

Chapter 11
Heaven

Chapter 11
Heaven

Heaven is a city 1500 miles each way and the height is the same as the sides. There is a heaven and there is a hell. In heaven there is no evil and no devil. One day we will enter heaven or hell. After hearing about hell, no one wants to miss heaven. Heaven is a prepared place for a prepared people. It is imperative that humans receive salvation or be born again to enter heaven. That is our passport to heaven. Our sacrifices on earth are little compared to the great gains in heaven. Everything there is completely available and free. Your name must be in the Lamb's Book of Life.

So much treasure is laid up in heaven. All desires are met. You will see the Glory of God. There are no tears, only joy beaming from every face. There is no darkness, only light. Jesus provides that eternal light. He is the Light of the world. There are no shadows in heaven. There is beautiful music and singing is heard, more beautiful than our earthly music. All spiritual bodies are so courteous, happy, and friendly. All are contented, never wanting to depart from heaven. In Jesus' presence is fullness of joy (Psalm 16:11).

Children aborted naturally and unnaturally are all in heaven nurtured by angels and women. Women that were unable to become pregnant will now love, nurture, and care for many infants and babies. Many angels also act as caretakers. These babies are so loved with great guidance.

The things we earthly people learned from the Holy Scriptures are now received with a depth of meaning. There are no churches there as they are not needed. There are many entrances to heaven where new spirits can enter their new homes. We all have a home ready for us furnished the way we each prefer. Only salvation has prepared us to live in this glory of heaven (John 3:3). Those that loved sin of pleasure on earth and whose name is not entered in the Book of Life wouldn't be able to survive heaven. Our memories will be freed from sorrow. Our soul will be filled with ecstasies of eternal life. When we enter heaven, we will be greeted by our spouse, parents, loved ones, family and friends that are there. The gates of heaven are many and are always open. The gates are one huge pearl studded with thousands of precious stones.

Everywhere are happy smiling souls. Many carrying and playing musical instruments, especially little harps. All string instruments are played by fingers instead of bows. Little children are taught to play their individual little harps. The varieties of food are so abundant. Trees have twelve different fruits and food on them. If any of the twelve foods fall to the ground and are not eaten, they just disappear. Remember nothing dies in heaven. People live forever. No marriages are made there. Earthly marriages now even become sweeter. Everyone has perfect contentment. God will use you with whatever talent you have. We will see and meet saints a thousand years old or a hundred years old, but they will look young. The water you drink is the water of life. Water fountains are everywhere with gold cups to drink from. This water revitalizes spirit people, and restores youth. Our bodies will be whole and will function perfectly. You'll never feel sick, weary, or die here. If you should feel weary, the water you drink revitalizes you. You won't grow older. Nothing decays or tarnishes. There is no dust, rain, cold, or hot. All weather is perfect. Our sight, hearing, speaking and memories will be perfect. What a blessing that will be for me. Able to recall everything. No obesity. No signs of the devil or evil. Beautiful lakes are everywhere. We will swim like fish under water and that water revitalizes us. Swans, birds, and fish are there.

There are mountains. If you prefer to live in mountains, your home will be there, or if you prefer water, your home will be by the water. Streets are gold, lined with beautiful stones and beautiful meadows, plains, parks, and forests are there. A majestic wall encircles the city of Jesus and God. God's throne is on a gentle slope. There is a temple, massive pillars, solid walls of unsullied pearl, great windows.

Jesus' glory is majestic and indescribable. He is full of love and a reflection of His Father's infinite love. His glory and majesty is indescribable. The nail holes in Jesus' hands and feet are large, very obvious. Saints and angels fall on their faces and worship Jesus.

I heard we will be surprised to see certain people in heaven and then again not find others you felt would be there. Jesus said he weeps when His children die and don't know or believe in Him. Even for the greatest sinners, Jesus would be willing to die again. That is the only reason I am writing this book, to let unbelievers know the truth about entering heaven. I don't want anyone to have to go to hell. The Bible says in John 8:32, "Then you will know the truth, and the truth will set you free." If only parents could see their children and how happy and joyful their life is in heaven they wouldn't grieve about their little ones, but make a strong desire to join them. I've read so often how angels or saints are carrying tiny infants and children pressed to their bosoms in love. They will grow to maturity in heaven. The children sing and dance and are never lonely or fearful. There are no tears in heaven, only joy, love, and peace. The children say they are anxious to see their parents, but have no desire to leave heaven.

God has a plan according to His purpose in each life. His purpose is to make each being into the image of His Son, Jesus Christ. Romans 8:6 says that the mind of sinful man is death, but the mind controlled by the Spirit is life and peace. The sinful mind is hostile to God, cannot please God. When saved, nothing in all creation will be able to separate us from the love of God that is in Christ Jesus our Lord. We hear about the Lamb's Book of Life. Our names must be written in this Book. As soon as you ask Jesus to forgive you of your sins and invite Jesus to live in your heart, your angels rush to heaven and record your name in this Lamb's Book of Life (Luke 10:20).

The whole atmosphere of heaven is filled with beautiful music. The flower colors are unbelievable. The flowers seem to sway with the music. If you stepped on one, they will spring right up. The smell in heaven is beautiful. I don't know if the flowers cause it but it is delightful many say. Happiness and joy beams from every face. You can see entire families together up there.

Your favorite animals can be in heaven. Here is a treasured story of our dog. I found a stray schnauzer dog wandering on the highway in the sleet and rain. I picked him up, called the radio and newspaper, placed ads but no one claimed him. We called him Chrissy because I found him at Christmas. We had another dog, Serje. Chrissy was so sweet. He was an older dog. He'd wait until Serje was not around then come to Ed or me to be held. Ed and I had been on a trip and our oldest son took care of the dogs. Chrissy had a kidney infection and became so ill the vet had to put him to sleep. It upset Eddie so much he was in tears about Chrissy's death. The night we returned home, Chrissy in a vivid dream came to my bedside. I patted and stroked him for some time. It felt so real then he flew up into the air, his hair flowing in the air. I feel he came to thank me and tell me goodbye.

Sometimes we can remember things way back fifty or sixty years, but usually, you remember some of the pain rather than the part the Lord wants you to remember. The Lord is going to surprise us with rewards even though the things we remember are painful, and even though we are not overcome by them or dwell on them. We do remember negative people in our lives, but we did much work for the Kingdom of God even if it was in hard situations. The Lord said He is giving rewards there.

I spoke about families in heaven. No marriages are made in heaven. Much time is spent in praying and magnifying our Lord and God. Songs on everyone's lips. When I was young, I wanted to be a singer. Now in my old age, I can barely make a sound. I blame it on my smoking for a long time. So I'm looking forward to being able to sing again. There will be no heartaches, no tragedies, no disasters or sorrow, no crying in heaven. I'm sure there will be tears of joy. Our earthly tears are stored in bottles with your names on them. The Bible says our angels collect our tears and store them. I'm sure my bottle is full as I weep with gratitude all the time. In my favorite Scripture, John 6:24, the Lord says,

"Is anything too difficult for our Lord? Pray, ask, believe and you'll receive." Then remember your prayer. Stay positive and receive . Be patient. God's timing is always right, but not always immediate.

I am reminded of how I would talk to Jesus and would tell Him that every picture I saw of Him is always so serious and solemn. I said, *I read of Your joy, happy and smiling face. So much I desire to see a picture of my smiling Jesus.* "You will fill me with joy in your presence, with eternal pleasures at your right hand" (Ps 16:11).

Around this time, I was attending a Women's Aglow meeting in Waynesboro. I was utterly amazed. When I walked in the room, they had beautiful portraits of Jesus laughing, head back, looking up with mouth open. The painter told the ladies how the Holy Spirit guided and directed her in painting Jesus' picture. The twinkling in His eyes and every feature. I bought several pictures. I have Jesus' portrait on the bureau beside Ed's picture. The two men I love the most. I always wear Ed's wedding ring and the cross of Jesus on a chain around my neck. I actually never remove it. I see the pictures when I go to bed and as I arise in the morning.

Jesus is the color of light and the Glory of God. Jesus is torn with compassion for those still on earth that do not believe or have received salvation. Remember John 3:3 says that you must be born again or saved to enter the gates of heaven. God so loved the world (all of us) that He gave his only begotten Son to die on the cross in dreadful suffering to cleanse us from all of our sins and qualify us to live in heaven with him, and all the saved people of the world and have everlasting life in love, peace and joy (John 3:16). God doesn't love us because we are valuable. His loving us makes us

Just this past Sunday, as I was finalizing my book, I had the deepest desire to include the Laughing Jesus picture in it. I only had the name "Sharol" written on the bottom of the Jesus picture. Was it a last name? Was it a man or woman? My daughter, Sue, said that she would try to get me information on her computer. She returned my call within minutes. Sharol Rosendahl, her address in Washington state, an artist, but no phone number. Sue emailed her for it. In moments, the phone rang and it was Sharol calling me. Miracle of miracles! She gave me her permission to use her picture, which she painted in two hours with spiritual guidance. We had the best conversation. Read Robert Liardon's book, *I Saw Heaven*. You'll appreciate the laughing picture of Jesus.

valuable. It is amazing how our Lord sees good things in us. Just know God loves each one of you so much. He has no favorites. So seek His will for yourself and be blessed. God is our greatest delight and His words our greatest treasure. Read the Scriptures I recorded and remember God's words are so powerful. He spoke the world into existence. Wow!

I once heard a story about a pastor in a small new England town. One Easter Sunday morning he came to the church carrying a rusty, bent, old bird cage and set it by the pulpit. Several eyebrows were raised and, as if in response, the pastor began to speak:

"I was walking through town yesterday when I saw a young boy coming toward me swinging this bird cage. On the bottom of the cage were three little wild birds, shivering with cold and fright. I stopped the lad and asked, 'What you got there son?'

'Just some old birds,' came the reply.

'What are you gonna do with them?' I asked.

'Take 'em home and have fun with 'em,' he answered. 'I'm gonna tease 'em and pull out their feathers to make 'em fight. I'm gonna have a real good time.'

'But you'll get tired of those birds sooner or later. What will you do then?'

'Oh, I got some cats,' said the little boy. 'They like birds. I'll take 'em to them.'

I was silent for a moment. 'How much do you want for those birds, son?'

'Huh??!!! Why, you don't want them birds, mister. They're just plain old field birds. They don't sing—they ain't even pretty!'

'How much?' I asked again.

The boy sized me up as if I were crazy and said, '$10?'

So I reached in my pocket and took out a ten dollar bill. I placed it in the boy's hand.

In a flash, the boy was gone.

I took the cage and gently carried it to the end of the alley where there was a tree and a grassy spot. Setting the cage down, I opened the door, and by softly tapping the bars persuaded the birds out, setting them free."

Well, that explained the empty bird cage on the pulpit, and then the pastor began to tell this story:

"One day satan and Jesus were having a conversation. Satan had just come from the Garden of Eden, and he was gloating and boasting. 'Yes, sir, I just caught the world full of people down there. Set me a trap, used bait I knew they couldn't resist. Got 'em all!'

'What are you going to do with them?' Jesus asked.

Satan replied, 'Oh, I'm gonna have fun! I'm gonna teach them how to marry and divorce each other. How to hate and abuse each other. How to drink and smoke and curse. I'm gonna teach them how to invent guns and bombs to kill each other. I'm really gonna have fun!'

'And what will you do when you get done with them?' Jesus asked.

'Oh, I'll kill 'em.' satan glared proudly.

'How much do you want for them?' Jesus asked.

'Oh, you don't want those people. They ain't no good. Why, you'll take them and they'll just hate you. They'll spit on, curse, and kill you! You don't want those people!'

'How much?' He asked again.

Satan looked at Jesus and sneered, 'All your tears, and all your blood.'

Jesus said, 'DONE!' Then He paid the price."

The pastor picked up the cage, he opened the door and he walked from the pulpit.

Isn't it funny how simple it is for people to trash God and then wonder why the world's going to hell? Isn't it funny how we believe what the newspapers say, but question what the Bible says? Isn't it funny how everyone wants to go to heaven provided they do not have to believe, think, say, or do anything the Bible says, or is it scary? Isn't it sad how someone can say "I believe in God" but still follow satan? Isn't it sad how you can send a thousand jokes through email and they spread like wildfire, but when you start sending messages regarding the Lord, people think twice about sharing? Isn't it sad how the lewd, crude, vulgar and obscene pass freely through cyber space, but the public discussion of Jesus is suppressed in the school and workplace? Isn't it sad how someone can be so fired up for Christ on Sunday, but be an invisible Christian the rest of the week? Isn't it sad how I can be more worried about what other people think of me than what God thinks of me?

We can be productive in this time of our life and see our ground enriched. He is putting miracles in our lives. The Lord says whatever we do in our life, think of eternal purposes and not just for this day.

Don't be afraid of heaven, but My reward is waiting for you (Rev. 22:12). I know you don't think of rewards, but there will be rewards for you. Your reward is laid up for you in heaven. His reward is waiting for me and for you, the reader. I'm reminded how Ed, my husband, was so ill with leukemia. He said he wasn't afraid to die and wasn't afraid of heaven, but that he was afraid to leave me. Ed was a part of my life since I was fourteen, all through high school, college and fifty-three years of married life. Yes, I am looking forward to seeing him and being with him again. Three years after Ed's death, God took my spirit to heaven to see Ed. I'd say once in a while, "I hope Ed is OK without me." We leaned on one another so often. I was sitting in heaven in what I would describe like a box car and Ed appeared at the open door of that car. He was so young, so happy, and had his arms outstretched. He came in and leaned down and gave me a sweet kiss on my lips, then backed out and returned to me again and gave me another kiss. When Ed leaned down that time, I could see out the door. I saw people with their backs to me, backed up to my building and seated in chairs and were all dressed alike. They were solidly seated as far as I could see to the horizon. It could have been millions of people. The chairs were all alike, their clothes all white, heads different colors. It was extremely bright and sunny in heaven. I didn't hear a sound except for myself saying, "Oh, Ed." I had asked the Lord just to see and that is what I got. I was so grateful for that. I thought afterward, "I know Ed kissed me, but I couldn't feel the pressure of his lips on mine. A couple days later, I had heard it said that you will know if an angel touches you, but you wouldn't feel the pressure from the touch. A spiritual being apparently has no earthly weight. We will find out one day. Make sure we are all ready for heaven. Jesus is the way, the truth and life and is the only way to heaven (John 14:6).

For an extended study on heaven, please consider these books:

1. *Come and See the Glory of God* by Mary Katherine Baxter.
2. *I Saw Heaven* by Roberts Liardon.
3. *My Dream of Heaven* by Rebecca Ruter Springer.
4. *Close Encounters of the God Kind* by Dr. Jesse Duplantis.
5. *Paradise, the Holy City and the Glory of the Throne* by Seneca Lordi.
6. *To Heaven and Back* by Rita Bennett.
7. *Caught Up Into Heaven* by Marietta Davis.

Chapter 12
Angels

Chapter 12
Angels

Ps 91:11 says if we make Jesus our protection, our shelter, then no harm will befall us. No disaster will come near our dwelling place. He commands His angels to guard us, protect us in all ways. The angels will lift us up in their hands. Ps 91 tells us that because we love the Lord, He will rescue, protect, and be with us in trouble.

I was visiting a church member at her home as she was ill and wanted to give her communion. I help the pastors by doing this. That day the streets and steps were coated in ice. I had to go up probably a dozen steps with no railing to hold onto. I prayed for the Lord to help me not to get hurt. I carefully got to the top, where I slipped and fell down backwards. As I was falling, I straightened out in the air, only backwards. I was hoping that not every bone in my body would be broken. Suddenly, I was standing upright at the bottom. I felt in complete shock, as I knew my angels caught me. Then I decided to go down an alley to her back door. I made it without slipping.

You can't see them, but you can sense or feel their presence. I can feel tingling in my hands as I reach up to them and I love that feeling. Also, as I lay in bed at night, I see movement all above me. I can't describe a being, but I surely see lots of movement and a pinpoint of light here and there. It brings me to joyful tears.

When I went out to the parking lot to get my car at the airport on returning home from a Christian Aglow convention in California, I found an inch of ice frozen on my windshield. Hagerstown had ice and snow storms. I couldn't see through the windshield so I had to turn the motor on and wait for it to defrost the ice. Suddenly a blond young man appeared in summer short sleeves in 20 degree weather. He had some sort of pick and was picking and breaking the ice. I had told my friend, Mildred, to wait over at the airport. I'd pick her up. Now I shouted, "You'll have to come here, I can't see through the windshield." We were dressed in summer clothes so I hurried to get inside the car. This kind man picked one side of the window and moved around to the other side. Mildred got in the car. I put down her window, leaned across Mildred and thanked this man profusely for removing the ice. He remarked he was glad to, and then he simply disappeared. No one else was in that parking lot, and my car was sitting alone. I asked the Lord if He had sent me an angel, and He said yes.

One Sunday in 1995 I was paralyzed. I couldn't move my arms, legs, or body. Ed got an ambulance, and they deposited me in the hospital. They said I'd have to wait till the next day to go down for x-rays. Early Monday morning a nurse came in and placed a water filled basin beside me on the bed and said, "Wash yourself." I thought how could I do that. I can't move. That nurse returned again and repeated "Wash yourself." and left the room. I said I would try. I moved my arms, sat up and washed myself. I stepped out of the bed and then got back in bed completely healed. Another nurse came in, and I said, "Do you want me to walk down for the x-ray or stay in the bed?" "You are paralyzed. There is no way you can get out of bed." I told her about the nurse that came in just before her. She said, "I am the first nurse, there isn't any other nurse." She inquired around, and no other nurse was there. It had to be an angel. How blessed I felt. I just kept praising the Lord.

Another similar incident happened. I was planning to go to Israel for a two week trip in 1999 with Pastor Sue and her church members. A week before we were to leave, I couldn't move my right leg at all. I called my son, Rob, and he had an ambulance come and they carried me down the steps. It seemed when I planned a Christian trip, the enemy would attack me. I stayed in the hospital for three days. The doctors felt it was a strange attack of arthritis. With nurses' manipulation and medication, I was back to normal. I took the trip to Israel. My granddaughter, Rebecca, joined me. One night we stayed at a camel farm. It was so different. Our entire group of about thirty people all slept under a huge tent on mattresses, men and women together in our travel clothes. The snoring was hilarious.

In the morning we were to take a camel caravan. Becca climbed with assistance up on a camel. They had a saddle on the camel to seat two people. Becca called, "Nanny, come ride with me." I had just been out of the hospital about five days so I was apprehensive about getting on a camel and then taking a caravan trip. I said, "Oh, Becca, I'm afraid to because of my leg." Becca called one of the head ladies over to pray that I could take the trip. At the very moment, I felt released of fear and got up on the rear seat. Becca turned around to check on me and said, "Nanny, look." I turned and there was a large group in a circle holding hands with bowed heads. I know I felt their prayers. I took the entire caravan and never had any trouble, not even a sore muscle from this incident. God is so dear, so sweet, and so kind. I thanked Him profusely with gratitude. In Luke 4:10 it is written, "He will command His angels concerning you to guard you carefully; they will lift you up in their hands, so that you will not strike your foot against a stone."

I was in Reading, Pennsylvania, attending a tennis match that one of my granddaughters was playing. It was getting so chilly, I decided to go to the car and get my jacket. As I got to the curb of the parking lot, I was looking for my daughter's car and tripped over the curb. I was outstretched in the air, falling, hoping every bone wouldn't be broken; and suddenly I was standing up. A dear angel caught me!

I'm reminded just last year our basement water tank stopped functioning and a new one was put in. The man that installed the tank and also took the old one out. I went down and just measured my water tank to be factual about the measurements. It also had water inside. He placed it on an open dolly to take it up the outside basement stairs, eighteen steps. I followed him because I felt he might need help getting it up all the stairs. He had it nearly to the top and it came loose and fell right down to where I was standing and absolutely stopped in front of me! It truly would have crushed me otherwise. The angels caught the tank and saved my life that day.

An even bigger event that my angels blessed me happened. I have a Vermont cart with bicycle wheels. I was trying to get my yard presentable for a garden club meeting. I had a truckload of tan bark delivered in my driveway to place around trees. The remainder of tan bark I loaded in my Vermont cart. It had rained and the tan bark was really wet. Great for placing around trees, but made the load extremely heavy. The cart was overloaded with the remaining bark. I could barely push the cart. I pushed it across the backyard and turned it to go down a rather steep hill. I realized I couldn't hold the cart, so I decided if I got in front of it, my body weight would support the cart. I faced the cart and turned it to the hill. It threw me down immediately, straight out with a big thump lying on my back. I put my legs up to stop the cart. Nothing touched me. I sat up and the cart was just sitting on the bank. I had to weep and really praised God. What a miracle! The loaded cart would have crushed me or broken both my legs.

I attended a church in Frederick as they have outstanding prophets, ministers, deliverers, evangelists in the world ministering. One spoke about the ministering angels that they are with, around all believers. They said that if we raised our hands up, in moments we would feel a moving sensation in the palms of our hand. I do that often, and I always feel a fuzzy, precious sensation which gives me such joy.

God really moves in when needed in any situation. One evening at one of our Bible study homes, I started to feel so warm and slightly dizzy. Then I felt a lovely cool breeze blow over me. At first I thought a door or window had been opened, but it was a heavenly breeze. I whispered, "Oh, Lord that feels so good. Please don't stop." It continued until I felt better. That was such a sweet blessing. That was either my angel or the Holy Spirit. I was blessed. I'm reminded of Psalm 91:11 where it says that He will command his angels concerning you to guard you in all your ways.

There are times when God has used us, the common man, to be helpers for Him. One time a name came to me repeatedly as I was driving to town. I said, "Okay, Lord. If this is from you, I'll go see her." I reversed my direction and drove out to her home. I found her standing at her back door weeping. She said she couldn't move and prayed for God to send an angel. I said this is the first time I've been called an angel. I got her to the kitchen table and some water to drink. We prayed for strength, healing and for feeling to return to her legs. The Lord strengthened her, so we moved to the living room to her favorite chair. I had visited and ministered to her times before being members of the same church. I had emphasized salvation, and she had received that, but refused Baptism of the Holy Spirit. As we settled on chairs, she said she wanted the baptism of the Holy Spirit. We did and she responded vigorously, and a joy appeared over her. We both felt blessed. She even received her spiritual language (tongues). The Lord strengthened her and her health improved.

Another similar incident happened. A name came to me repetitiously that was in the hospital. So I said I'd go see if I could help them. I was able to park in the hospital parking area and was walking on the pavement to the entrance. There is a bench there, and a man was sitting there bent over in agony. I stopped and said, "Are you alright?" He said, "I don't know where the front door is." I said I'd take him and then he said, "I can't stand up." I said, "I believe in prayer. Can I pray for you?" He said alright. Then after prayer he straightened up and was able to walk with me to the front desk. They took over, so I visited the person I had come to see. He was fine and preparing to leave the hospital. I realized the Lord can move in strange ways. I was so grateful to be used.

Here is another story. I was flying to Boston to visit my ill sister, Katherine. This was my first trip alone since Ed died. He always led and I followed. Our plane landed at Harrisburg to change planes. I got off the plane and got on the ground floor escalator following the crowd. A lady stepped upon the escalator by my side and inquired where I was going. I told her and she said to follow her. We got off the escalator and walked back to the counter I needed for my next flight. She took me to the counter. I was looking for my ticket and then looked up to thank her and she had disappeared. I realized she was an angel. I was so grateful and blessed.

One night as I was getting into bed, I remembered that I had left my car trunk open. I knew by morning my battery would be dead, but I just could not go back down the stairs to close it, as I was recuperating from a hip replacement. As I was considering calling someone to come close it for me, I decided instead to ask my angel to close it. In the morning I went down the stairs and out to check the car. The trunk was closed! Praise God!

A neighbor called frantically one day saying her little son was locked in the bathroom. He had locked the door and couldn't open it. Ed was mowing the lawn so I stopped him. We prayed over the situation and Ed went next door. He took hold of the knob and the door opened. All of us were so shocked. Ed said we prayed and the Lord opened it. We hoped this caused her to realize what a great God we have.

One summer many years ago Ed took me and my sister, Katherine, to swim in a supposedly bottomless lake. We swam out to a floating raft. Katherine dove off the raft, went under the water and didn't come up. Ed dove in and found Katherine swimming down instead of up to the surface. Ed retrieved her and brought her to the surface. I feel Ed saved Katherine's life. She just died this past year and is missed by all our families.

When I visit the sick in my church or the infirmed, I frequently take a little gift of an angel. I took a sweet angel to a lady, and she said she placed the angel in a window in her house that never had the sun shine through. After the angel was placed there, the sun shined through that window. If she had to go to the hospital, she always took the angel as it was special to her.

A genuine encounter with a holy angel glorifies God not the angel. We are never to worship our angels. Angels guard us, deliver us from harm, meet our needs and carry out God's purposes for us. They worship God (Psalm 91:15). God is with us in trouble.

Conclusion

Conclusion

When God spoke to me in heaven in a dream vision, He raised His hands straight up and came forward to me. In a loud voice, He said, "I want the last chapter of your book to have the plan of salvation. I want everyone to be in heaven with me." That is what gave me the only desire to write this book. That is where my heart is. I want everyone to be in heaven.

This plan of salvation is the greatest miracle available to the entire world. This is our guarantee of entering heaven and being with God and Jesus forever. Living with all Christians.

If satan has you bound, break his power (Matthew 12:28 – 16:19). Command him to let you go and never to return. Then claim deliverance, healing, and release from all evil in the name of Jesus Christ. Cover yourself with the protecting Blood of Jesus. "I tell you the truth, my Father will give you whatever you ask in my name" (John 16:23). Ask Father and receive joy complete. Remember heaven is so beautiful, no suffering, no sickness and no death, only joy and love. 1,000 years in heaven seems like one day on earth. 1 Peter 5:10 says that after you have suffered, God will restore you, make you strong, firm and steadfast. He will lift you up right out of all sin. He'll lift you up to heavenly places where Jesus lives. Then you will see God face to face. You'll feel His abiding presence. You are precious in the sight of our God. He'll say "My child, come home." Jesus has given His Word that He'll never leave or forsake us. His Word is as firm as His character. We'll go to heaven in love to please and glorify God with the many holy angels. John 14:1-3 says that our greatest treasures are His Words. When Jesus returns, evil will be destroyed. Jesus will release us from anything the enemy had control of. We will be free of worries, sickness, fears, money, jobs, economic problems, or conditions. The earth will become a planet of peace (Isaiah 51:11). Jesus has such compassion for those who haven't received Him as their Savior that He would be willing to give His life again on the cross. Take this time to pray to our Lord and Savior, the greatest Friend you'll ever have. Believe these words with your heart and you will be born again and qualified for heaven.

Pray this prayer:

"Jesus, come into my life. Forgive me of all my sins. Cleanse my heart. Make me a new person in You right now. I do believe You are the Son of God and that you gave your Life on the cross for me. Jesus, thank you for loving me enough to die for me. I receive you as my Savior and Lord. Please come into my life and my heart. Never leave me. In Your Name I pray."

Congratulations! Your are a new creature in Christ. Old things are passed away. Behold all things are become new (2 Cor. 5:17).

LaVergne, TN USA
17 November 2010
205293LV00002B/88/P

9 780982 798041